THE
FETAL RIGHT *to* LIFE ARGUMENT

SECOND EDITION, 2020

C. Paul Smith

Archway Publishing books may be ordered through booksellers or by contacting:

Archway Publishing
1663 Liberty Drive
Bloomington, IN 47403
www.archwaypublishing.com
844-669-3957

Interior and Cover Image Credit: C. Paul Smith

Scripture quoted from the King James Version of the Bible.

ISBN: 978-1-4808-9600-0 (sc)
ISBN: 978-1-4808-9602-4 (hc)
ISBN: 978-1-4808-9601-7 (e)

Library of Congress Control Number: 2020917625

Print information available on the last page.

Archway Publishing rev. date: 11/13/2020

Contents

Preface

The *Roe v. Wade* case from 1973 (410 U.S. 113) is probably the best known and most important Supreme Court case in the last fifty years. It has affected how the Constitution is interpreted; it has been the foundation for changes in our laws and in societal morality; it has divided the nation on moral issues; and it continues to be a lightning rod in political debate.

As a law student, I did a research project on *Roe v. Wade*, which resulted in the book *The Fetal Right to Life Argument* (1977). The contents of that book continue to be pertinent and helpful today. I have republished that book in 2020, with significant revisions and updates that include many of the subsequent Supreme Court cases that have interpreted, modified, and extended *Roe v. Wade*. Because of the continuing importance of this case, and because the original case is so frequently misrepresented, this book will be helpful to those who really want to understand the *Roe v. Wade* case.

Roe v. Wade is a complex case that brought several very significant results—some good and some bad. The case established a woman's right to privacy and a right to control her own body. This is good. The case also firmly established the right and power of the Supreme Court to recognize some inalienable rights that had not previously been established. This is also good, and it reaffirms the Ninth Amendment—the fact that a right has not previously been enumerated does not mean that such a right does not exist. This is a significant matter, and it continues to be debated and modified as the Supreme Court wrestles with when and how to establish rights that have not previously been recognized (e.g., homosexual conduct and same-sex marriage). While the Supreme Court may have erred in recognizing some new rights, nevertheless, I contend that the right and power to do this is unquestionably invested in the Supreme Court by the Constitution.

But there are some other aspects of *Roe v. Wade* that were clearly wrong. First, the case extinguished the fetal right to life. In my opinion, this was a colossal error, a lack of judicial restraint, an abuse of judicial power, an act of social activism, and an act of judicial legislation. There was no need for the Supreme Court to invalidate the laws of most of the states on the abortion issue. Second, the case was an unprovoked and improper attack on federalism, as the Supreme Court took from the states—usurped—the right of the states to legislate on matters of sexual relations, procreation, and fetal rights. Whether or not the Supreme Court got this right, it is nevertheless indisputable that *Roe v. Wade* has wrought a total overhaul on federalism and individual rights under the Constitution. Finally, the standard established by the Supreme Court in *Roe v. Wade* for when and how a state can prohibit abortions was ambiguous, conflicting, and confusing from the very beginning, and it has continued to be litigated for forty-seven years since the case was decided.

With this backdrop, I invite you to read the following analysis of the *Roe v. Wade* decision and come to appreciate the serious problems created by it.

Roe v. Wade has now become an integral part of American law. As a nation, it seems that even those who disagree with parts of it have resigned themselves to accept it. Even those who disagree with *Roe* have mostly stopped fighting it and no longer seek to have it changed through a constitutional amendment or through court cases. But it is nevertheless important for God-fearing people to recognize that the Supreme Court made a terrible mistake in *Roe v. Wade*. It is important that Christians and other religious people recognize the evil that has triumphed because of *Roe*. The *Roe v. Wade* case has infected our laws with an evil virus that is now firmly embedded in our Constitution.

We must never forget the moral degradation that was injected into our laws by this case. God-fearing people should continue to be repulsed by the bad parts of the *Roe* case. Extinguishing the fetal right to life is not only an afront to God, but it is depraved and horrific. We should never forget this. In doing so, we would become weak and docile lemmings, willing to blithely go along with whatever laws a court might enact, happily subjecting to an evil standard as if there was nothing wrong with it. Unfortunately, this is what has happened. Tolerance has become acceptance, and acceptance has now become embracement. The words of Alexander Pope have been fulfilled—a vice that was once opprobrious to almost everyone now seems to be embraced by almost all:

> Vice is a monster of so frightful mien,
> As, to be hated, needs but to be seen;
> Yet seen to oft, familiar with her face,
> We first endure, then pity, then embrace.
> —Alexander Pope, *Essay on Man* (1733)

In speaking out against abortion on demand and against major parts of the *Roe v. Wade* case, I am not calling for any actions of violent protest against Planned Parenthood or other abortion clinics, nor against any of the people who provide abortion services or who encourage or participate in abortions. I do not want to be a part of any of this. God can extract whatever justice may be requisite, and He can do it on His timetable. But my purpose is to awaken God-fearing people to the grave evil that America and the world have embraced by legalizing most abortions and extinguishing the fetal right to life. If society has fallen to the level where the flaws in *Roe* cannot be corrected, then we may have to suffer and survive the best we can under a bad law. I don't want to send my grandchildren to school to have them every day confront or be confronted by those who embrace *Roe*. Proper opposition can be handled in another way. Sometimes we have to submit to wrongs without fighting.

But it is of supreme importance that we recognize the great evil in unwarranted abortions, that we not lose an abhorrence for them.

It is from this perspective that I present *The Fetal Right to Life Argument.* The Supreme Court made a grave error when it extinguished the fetal right to life through its *Roe v. Wade* decision. The good parts of *Roe,* including recognizing a woman's right to privacy, did not have to come at the expense of the fetal right to life. All in all, there are several serious legal and moral problems that *Roe v. Wade* has established in American law. Those who continue to work to correct these problems should be commended and supported. And we must never fail to realize how the termination of unborn human life without proper justification is a grievous sin, whether or not society now celebrates it to be a cherished right. Woe to any society that celebrates this perversion as being good.

A lot of people won't like this book. And a lot of them won't like me. And if you agree with this book, they won't like you either. But it doesn't matter. This book states things that need to be said. Just as the story of the Holocaust needs to be told (where six million Jews were exterminated by the Nazis between 1941 and 1945), so must the elimination of the fetal right to life be told. The pro-choice/pro-life debate that has now engulfed the nation for fifty years continues to be polarizing and divisive. If you let it be known where you stand on this issue, you will be embraced by some and rejected by others. Maybe you can keep secret your feelings on this issue. But then you would not be a courageous advocate for truth and righteousness.

The Guttmacher Institute reports that worldwide there have been fifty-six million induced abortions each year from 2010 to 2014.[1] In America, the number for 2017 is 862,320. Guttmacher further reports that worldwide, 25 percent of pregnancies end in abortion. This situation is not good; it's not right.

The grievous mistakes made by the Supreme Court should be

---

[1] https://www.guttmacher.org/fact-sheet/induced-abortion-worldwide (accessed April 13, 2020).

exposed and remembered. And the millions of fetal deaths that have been authorized and promoted and celebrated because of *Roe v. Wade* should be remembered. We must never forget.

We must never forget or fail to understand the serious legal mistakes and the degraded moral standard established by the United States Supreme Court in its *Roe v. Wade* decision. The Court's opinion in *Roe* was complicated, and it included some parts that were good and correct. But the part that held that a human fetus does not have a right to life—that part was wrong, and it was based upon legally flawed arguments, and it was an unconstitutional usurpation of power by the Supreme Court. The failure of the Supreme Court to appropriately protect the fetal right to life was a moral travesty that has given a stamp of approval for the barbaric and evil practice of killing unborn babies. To a nation, many of whom are determined to divorce themselves from God, they continue to herald the *Roe v. Wade* decision as their savior. But the God in heaven weeps at the gross wickedness of those who regard unborn human life as dross and who fail to appreciate and cherish the sanctity of human life and the means by which children are conceived and brought into the world.

It has been almost fifty years since the Supreme Court announced its ruling in *Roe v. Wade*. Much of America, perhaps half of America, has just accepted the *Roe* case and moved on. But while there are some good parts of that decision, the egregious flaws in *Roe* must be acknowledged and never forgotten. If America comes to accept the *Roe* case as the standard for what is moral and right, then this will corrupt our moral compass and contribute to separating us from God's point of view about abortion. God does not endorse abortion on demand; it is reprehensible to Him. God-fearing people should never relinquish or abandon God's moral standards, and, when possible, they should continue to work to correct the serious problems created by *Roe*.

This book is written to help people understand the serious mistakes and flaws in the seminal *Roe v. Wade* case.

CHAPTER ONE

The Roe v. Wade Decision

For more than one hundred years, until 1967, almost every state had laws protecting human life from conception. Between 1967 and 1972, seventeen states passed laws legalizing abortion, while thirty-three states retained laws that protected fetal life. In 1972, New York voted to repeal its legalized abortion law, but Governor Nelson Rockefeller vetoed the repeal. On January 22, 1973, the Supreme Court of the United States handed down its decision in *Roe v. Wade*, 410 U.S. 113 (1973), which invalidated the laws in the thirty-three states that protected fetal life from conception.[2] The Court held that a woman's right to privacy would be violated if she were not allowed to abort the living, unborn child within her. The Supreme Court characterized this as a "fundamental right" that can only be limited for "compelling reasons."[3] While the court did say that the state had a right to protect fetal life in the last trimester

---

[2] The Supreme Court also addressed abortion issues in the companion case of *Doe v. Bolton*, 410 U.S. 179 (1973). In that case, the court struck down a Georgia law that permitted abortions only in accredited hospitals, requiring the authorization of the hospital staff plus three other doctors, and limiting the procedure to only Georgia residents.

[3] 410 U.S. 155, 163-164; see also *Akron v. Akron Center for Reproductive Health*, 462 U.S. 416, 420 (1983); and *Webster v. Reproductive Health Services*, 492 U.S. 490, 520 (1989).

of pregnancy, the Court denied that the fetus has any enforceable right to life. The Court gave no rational explanation of why existing laws that protected human life from conception were erroneous or unreasonable, except that it is difficult to determine when conception occurs and that a human fetus is not a "person" within the meaning of the Fourteenth Amendment (410 U.S. 157). Because the Court could find no constitutional provision explicitly protecting the fetal right to life, it invalidated those state laws that did provide such protection. The court did not consider whether the pregnancy was voluntarily induced.

Since the woman's right to privacy is a fundamental right, that right can only be limited for compelling reasons, such as the state's right to protect women and to protect viable fetal life (410 U.S. 155, 163–164). The Court said that no regulations on abortions were permissible in the first three months (trimester) of a pregnancy (410 U.S. 164). In the second three months, the Court said that a state may prohibit or regulate abortions in order to protect the life of the pregnant woman (410 U.S. 163–164). In the final three months of pregnancy, the Court said that a state could regulate and prohibit abortions either to protect the pregnant woman or to protect the potential human life within the woman (410 U.S. 163–164).

As a result of *Roe v. Wade*, no unborn child has any right to live or to be born. Each state may, if it chooses, protect fetal life and prohibit abortions in the last three months of pregnancy (or when the fetus reaches the stage of viability), but at no time is the fetus itself recognized as possessing the right to live.

The Court undoubtedly felt it had navigated the wisest route by holding that the responsibility for deciding whether to have an abortion should be left with each individual woman. By establishing such a standard, the Court undoubtedly felt it had avoided the establishment of any religious belief on the subject and had put the total burden and responsibility on the pregnant woman for the consequences of her decision.

As far as the pregnant woman is concerned, the *Roe* decision is perfectly fair. But the Court glossed over the issue of whether the unborn have a right to life. The *Roe* decision is unfair to unborn children. It is inconsistent to say that the state has a right in the fetus's life, while the fetus itself has no such right. Yet that is what the Court said. If any entity has an interest in a fetus's life, the fetus itself certainly has. Abortion is distinguishable from contraception—"prevention of conception"; abortion terminates a living human fetus.

Curiously, the Court in *Roe* said that it "need not resolve the difficult question of when life begins," 410 U.S. 159. Yet *Roe* clearly establishes that the right to life does not begin until birth. The Court's attempt to avoid this issue is most unsatisfactory. There is no question biologically or medically that life exists from conception. The Court presumed that the right to life could not possibly exist before the fetus is quickened (becomes viable). But they were unsure of this as well, so they left it to each state to protect viable fetuses, if they so desire. There is no logical basis for saying that the *right to life* does not exist until a living human fetus reaches a certain stage in its development. How easily *Roe* could have been decided more fairly if the court had recognized that the *right to life* coexists with *life* itself. But by focusing primarily on the woman's privacy right, the court felt quite comfortable with its decision (a seven-to-two vote[4]). The court did say that if it could be established that a fetus is a "person" within the meaning of the Fourteenth Amendment, then abortion could be constitutionally prohibited. But the court could find no legal support for this position and accordingly held that state laws prohibiting abortion impinge upon a woman's right of privacy over her own body.

The court could easily have found that the fetal right to life exists under the Fifth, Ninth, Tenth, and Fourteenth Amendments. But the

---

[4] Justice Blackmun authored the opinion. He was joined by Chief Justice Burger and by Justices Douglas, Brennan, Stewart, Marshall, and Powell. Justices White and Rehnquist dissented.

court said that in the absence of such a right being explicitly written in the Constitution, such a right cannot exist (410 U.S. 156-58). It is interesting to note, though, that the pregnant woman's privacy right to have an abortion is not explicitly listed in the Constitution. This did not prevent the court from finding it to be constitutionally protected. One of the purposes of the Ninth Amendment is to protect inalienable, God-given rights, which may not have been enumerated in the Constitution. The Court in *Roe* has adopted an obvious double standard by relying on the Fifth, Ninth, and Fourteenth Amendments to find the woman's privacy right but refusing to apply the same principles to recognize the fetal right to life.

Lest there be any doubt, the scholarship of Justice Blackmun's majority opinion in *Roe* was widely regarded as inferior jurisprudence. As Ann Coulter described: "No one talks about the 'legal analysis' in *Roe*, because there is none. Liberals wanted abortion, so they discovered a right to it."[5] Coulter also wrote this:

> Harvard law professor—and Watergate special prosecutor—Archibald Cox said of the opinion in *Roe*, "Neither historian, nor layman, nor lawyer will be persuaded that all the prescriptions of Justice Blackmun are part of the Constitution." Stanford Law School dean John Hart Ely said *Roe* "is not constitutional law and gives almost no sense of an obligation to try to be." Harvard law professor Laurence Tribe has said that "the substantive judgment on which it rests is nowhere to be found." Even Ruth Bader Ginsburg has called *Roe* an act of "heavy-handed judicial intervention" and ridiculed the opinion during her confirmation hearings.[6]

---

[5] Ann Coulter, *Godless—The Church of Liberalism* (New York: Crown Publishing Group, 2006), p. 92.

[6] Coulter, p. 92.

Over time, *Roe v. Wade* had a transformative impact on the entire world. The US took the lead in disrespecting and disregarding fetal life, while initially much of the world continued to protect the unborn. Within a two-year period (1973–1975), the highest courts in the United States, Austria, Canada, France, Italy, and West Germany ruled on abortion statutes. The high court in Austria ruled that unborn children were not persons protected by their national constitution until after the first three months of pregnancy. The high courts in France and Italy upheld laws that proscribed abortion except when the mother's health was endangered. In March 1975, the Supreme Court of Canada was confronted with a law prohibiting abortion except when continued pregnancy would be likely to endanger the mother's health. The court unanimously held that no case had been presented requiring constitutional examination. The chief justice said that regulation of abortion was a legislative matter. In West Germany, the high court ruled that unborn children enjoy constitutional protection at all stages of pregnancy. It is interesting to note that in 1976, of these six nations, the United States afforded the least protection to fetal life.[7] But it was not long thereafter that abortion became legal in all of these nations.

Roe is now history. But it is profitable to discuss what the Court could have done, or should have done, in the context of correcting the unjust law that was brought about by *Roe*. The Court made it clear that if a fetal right to life existed, some antiabortion statutes would be constitutional. But because the Supreme Court says it can find no such right in the Constitution, it is necessary to explicitly put one there if such a right is to be protected in America.

---

[7] John D. Gorby, "Introduction to the Translation of the Abortion Decision of the Federal Constitutional Court of the Federal Republic of Germany," *The John Marshall Journal of Practice and Procedure* 9 (1976): 558–561.

CHAPTER TWO

The Fetal Right to Life That the Court Could Not Find

The basic issue in *Roe v. Wade* is not whether a woman has a right to terminate her pregnancy but, rather, whether the Constitution prohibits the protection of her unborn offspring.[8] The

---

[8] Robert A. Destro characterizes the *Roe* decision as follows:

> In the course of its opinion in *Roe v. Wade* the Supreme Court recognized that a woman's right to terminate her pregnancy, whether based upon the right to privacy or some other constitutional right, is contingent upon a prior finding that her unborn offspring has no constitutionally protected right to life. Relying upon an analysis of the constitutional usage of the word "person," while also citing a lack of 19th century common law protection for the unborn, the Court ruled that the unborn are not "persons" within the meaning of the due process clause of the fourteenth amendment and, thus, not entitled to the right to life....
>
> The reasoning of the Court has been examined and found to be wanting legally, historically, scientifically, and philosophically. The basic issue in the abortion cases was not whether a woman has a right to terminate her pregnancy, but rather, whether or not the Constitution forbids the protection of her unborn offspring. The Court did not discuss the issue.

Court focused almost exclusively on women's rights and refused to discuss the issue of fetal rights, except to say that a fetus is not a person within the meaning of the Fourteenth Amendment. It does not follow, however, that because a fetus is not a "person" under the Fourteenth Amendment that it is not in fact a person or that it does not have a right to life. The Court's decision has a number of flaws that misled it to conclude that it need not decide whether there exists a fetal right to life.

A. Lack of Judicial Restraint

This problem of lack of judicial restraint is mentioned first because it is at the root of all the other problems. For some reason—eagerness, a sense of urgency, or whatever—the Court took upon itself the responsibility to set forth new principles of law regulating abortion. The Court's trimesters of pregnancy scheme is clearly an example of judicial legislation. This becomes especially apparent when you examine the facts of the conflict before the Court. Texas claimed the right to protect all unborn children from the moment of conception,

Both aspects of the holdings in the abortion cases have come under attack by the introduction of various proposals for constitutional amendments. If passed, these proposals would either reverse or substantially modify the decisions in *Roe v. Wade* and *Doe v. Bolton* [companion case to *Roe*]. The proposals merit serious and careful consideration, for they present two issues which are of vital importance to any efficient resolution of the abortion controversy: (1) The extent to which unborn human life is to be considered a value deserving of constitutional protection; and (2) the extent to which the states, as sovereign governmental units, are to be permitted to promulgate reasonable regulations to protect the public health and the welfare of women seeking abortions.

... Indeed, *Roe v. Wade* and *Doe v. Bolton* raise more questions than they resolve ....The controversy is as complex as it is volatile and it will clearly not "go away" if ignored. (Robert A. Destro, "Abortion and the Constitution: The Need for a Life-Protective Amendment," *California L. Rev.* 63 [1975]: 1250, 1340–1341) except when the health of the mother was endangered. Jane Roe claimed that she had a complete right of privacy over her own body such that she could have an abortion at any time she wanted. The Court rejected the contentions of both parties and pronounced a new rule in between the extremes sought by the two parties. Rather than dismissing Jane Roe's claim and/or invalidating the Texas statute, the Court decided to take on the whole abortion question. The Court-promulgated law in *Roe* was far broader than was necessary to resolve the conflict before the Court. Even if the Texas law was invalid, the Court had no authority to promulgate a whole new abortion regulation for the nation. If the statute in question was unconstitutional, the Court should have invalidated it. But the Constitution gives the judicial branch no right to make law; it reserves that right to the legislatures.[9] Further, as Justice Rehnquist stated in his dissent in *Roe*, the Court erred by "formulat[ing] a rule of constitutional law broader than is required by the precise facts to which it is to be applied" (J. Rehnquist, dissenting in *Roe v. Wade*, 410 U.S. at 172).[10] The Court's judicial legislation has serious deficiencies, which can be corrected only by the Court overruling itself or by congressional legislation. The Court clearly acted outside the scope of its delegated authority, and being the Court of "last resort," which it is, there exists no normal procedure to review its decision. These problems can be corrected only by a constitutional amendment.

When the system of checks and balances was made a part of our

---

[9] Justice Brandeis articulated reasons and principles for limiting those actions that the Supreme Court should take in exercising judicial review. Some of those reasons include the following: "The Court will not formulate a rule of constitutional law broader than is required by the precise facts to which it is to be applied." He also said: "When the validity of an act of the Congress is drawn in question, and even if a serious doubt of constitutionality is raised, it is a cardinal principle that this Court will first ascertain whether a construction of the statute is fairly possible by which the question may be avoided." Justice Brandeis, concurring opinion, *Ashwander v. TVA*, 297 U.S. 288, 346–348 (1936).

[10] Judge Rehnquist was citing *Liverpool, New York and Philadelphia Steamship Co. v. Commissioners of Emigration*, 113 U.S. 33, 39 (1885).

Constitution, Congress was given the responsibility to make laws, and the Court was given the responsibility to invalidate those laws that, when contested, were found to violate the Constitution. What has happened in this case is the exact, fundamental error that our Constitution was intended to guard against: the law-making body should not be the one to say whether its law does or does not violate the Constitution. If the Court makes a law, who is there to review its validity? Only the Court itself. The Court becomes a law unto itself, with no one in a position to review its doings. This situation is quite different from the normal procedure where the Court reviews laws made by Congress. A law enacted by Congress must go through extensive hearings and discussion, be approved by both Houses of Congress, and then approved by the President of the United States before it becomes law. But the Court followed no such rigorous and demanding procedure in creating the three-trimester regulation approach to abortion announced in *Roe*.

Considering all the uncertainties involved with abortion and the many abortion laws that had been undergoing change, it was inappropriate for the Court to thrust its legislative-type solution out of the clear blue sky for questions that had not been briefed or argued before the Court.

Mr. Justice Black, who dissented in *Griswold v. Connecticut*, 381 U.S. 479 (1965), warned that overactivism by the Court would jeopardize the balance of powers in our three-branch government.[11] He

---

[11] Justice Black wrote:

> The adoption of ... a loose, flexible, uncontrolled standard for holding laws unconstitutional, if ever it is achieved, will amount to a great unconstitutional shift of power to the courts which I believe and am constrained to say will be bad for the courts and worse for the country. Subjecting federal and state laws to such an unrestrained and unrestrainable judicial control as to the wisdom of legislative enactments would, I fear, jeopardize the separation of governmental powers ....
>
> I realize that many good and able men have eloquently spoken and written, sometimes in rhapsodical strains, about the duty of this

advocated amending the Constitution as the appropriate method for resolving new questions of law. Admittedly, the executive or judiciary branches could resolve problems quicker than the legislative branch, but in spite of this problem of delay, the Constitution prescribes that in this democracy, laws are to be made by the legislature—not the judiciary.

In the 1976 death penalty cases, the Supreme Court indicated that moral values may be properly imposed by legislatures but not by the courts: "[I]n a democratic society, legislatures—not courts—are constituted to respond to the will and consequently the moral values of the people."[12] Perhaps *Roe* would have been decided differently by the Supreme Court today. But the *Roe* decision need not remain in force. The fetal right-to-life legislation that was necessitated by *Roe*, if successful, can eradicate the unfair results of *Roe*.

One of the curious things about *Roe* is the near unanimity of the Court. One cannot help but wonder whether the Court was aware of more than a few arguments in favor of the fetal right to life. Had the Court invited comments and arguments on its proposed new regulations before officially issuing its opinion, perhaps the outcome would have been different. But, of course, the Supreme Court is not accustomed to rulemaking and legislating. But then again, it is not supposed to legislate. And its lack of restraint in this case led it to promulgate a law fraught with problems and unanswered questions.

Court to keep the Constitution in tune with the times. [I] must with all deference reject that philosophy. The Constitution makers knew the need for change and provided for it. Amendments suggested by the people's elected representatives can be submitted to the people or their selected agents for ratification. That method of change was good for our founding Fathers, and being somewhat old-fashioned I must add it is good enough for me. 381 U.S. 521–522.

[12] Chief Justice Burger, dissenting opinion, *Gregg v. Georgia*, 426 U.S. 153, 175 (1976), quoting from *Furman v. Georgia*, 408 U.S. 238, 383 (1972).

B. Due Process Rights of the Pregnant Woman

Because women were not given an unlimited right over their bodies, some will argue that *Roe* unduly restricts a woman's due process rights. But the practical effect of *Roe* comes close to giving her unlimited control. Actually, the Court bestowed more rights on women than due process required. In *Eisenstadt v. Baird*, 405 U.S. 438 (1972), the Court held that "it is the right of the individual, married or single, to be free from unwarranted governmental intrusion into matters so fundamentally affecting a person as the decision whether to bear or beget a child" (405 U.S. at 453). However, the Court did not say that this right superseded the fetal right to life. Governmental intrusion is warranted to protect the defenseless unborn children. The unfettered right to decide whether to beget a child ends where the fetal right to life begins. Because the Court refused to find a fetal right to life, it felt it could extend the right to decide whether to bear and beget children to include the right to abort a live human fetus. The Court based its holding on the reasoning that pregnant women have a right to privacy over their bodies and that laws prohibiting abortion violate their Fourteenth Amendment "due process" rights.[13] This reasoning totally fails to consider whether or not the pregnancy was voluntarily induced. If it was, then by denying her an abortion, she cannot contend that her due process rights have been violated, for she voluntarily became pregnant. The counter argument to this is that if the fetus has no rights, then the question of voluntariness is irrelevant. However, this presumes that fetuses have no rights, which is the ultimate question. The validity of the Court's conclusion that a woman's right to have an abortion rests upon her due process

---

[13] One constitutional law scholar commented that the question is not "How can we justify abortion?" but "How can we justify compulsory child bearing?" Gerald Gunther, "The Supreme Court 1971 Term Forward: In Search of Evolving Doctrine on a Changing Court: A Model for a New Equal Protection," 86 *Harvard L. Rev.* 1, 35 (November 1972). Such a phrasing of the question avoids the basic question of whether the fetus has a right to life. If the fetus has this right, then in the absence of extenuating circumstances, the woman should be compelled to bear the child she voluntarily initiated.

rights assumes that the fetus has no right to life. Thus, the Court could not rationally conclude that the privacy right exists without first determining whether the fetal right to life exists. The Court thought it could logically avoid this question, but as was mentioned earlier, this is a basic flaw in the Court's opinion.

In holding that antiabortion statutes violate a woman's right to privacy under the due process clause of the Fourteenth Amendment, the Court made an obvious extension of the meaning of that amendment. When the Fourteenth Amendment due process clause became a part of the Constitution in 1868, at least thirty of the thirty-seven states had already enacted statutes prohibiting abortion.[14] The Fourteenth Amendment was not intended to invalidate these antiabortion statutes. The Court in *Roe* obviously extended the meaning of this amendment beyond what it was originally intended to do. The plain meaning of this amendment would seem to protect unborn human beings, rather than create a right in women to kill unborn children with impunity.[15]

1. *Extension of parental responsibility.* Laws exist requiring parents to care for their children after birth at the risk of criminal or civil penalties if they fail to do so. Parents have this responsibility because it is universally recognized that without help, even healthy newborn babies cannot survive. The same rationale that limits parents' rights, requiring them to provide for their helpless babies, is the reason why a pregnant woman does not have the right to terminate the life of the individual within her, whose life is totally dependent upon her until

---

[14] Thirty states and six territories that had antiabortion statutes in 1868 are listed in 410 U.S.113, 175–176 (Rehnquist, J., dissenting), note 1. Twenty-one of those statutes were still in effect in 1970.

[15] While the court did not feel that a human fetus was a "person" within the meaning of the Fourteenth Amendment, it nevertheless says that corporations are persons for Fourteenth Amendment purposes. *Santa Clara County v. Southern Pac. R. R.,* 118 U.S. 394 (1886). Perhaps by incorporating all fetuses, they could be recognized as possessing the right to life.

birth. No one's rights are unlimited. A basic tenet of all law is that no one has a right to infringe upon the rights of another person. One of the main purposes of laws requiring couples to be legally married *before* having sexual intercourse is to ensure that parents nourish and care for their offspring from the moment of conception.[16] Just as parents have no right to allow or cause their children to be injured after birth, neither is it logical that they should be allowed to kill their unborn, living children. Our marriage laws were intended to protect both born and unborn children. Because parents initiate their children's lives, the law has historically held parents responsible to care for both their born and unborn children. The Court in *Roe* has now undermined this fundamental principle of law. Henceforth, what rational basis can the Court give for prohibiting intercourse before marriage? If born children were always meant to be the only children with the right to life, then why have our laws prohibited extramarital sex for so many years? The Court could have easily found the fetal right to life to be implicitly protected by the Constitution through the Ninth and Tenth Amendment in the laws of every state that prohibits extramarital sex and make parents responsible for their children.

2. *Personal rights are not absolute.* No personal right is absolute, either to the extent of infringing upon other's rights or to the extent of harming one's self. Suicide statutes are an example of this. Also, there are laws to protect those who are mentally and physically handicapped. Many examples exist of women who suffer serious mental and physical aftereffects from abortions, even when performed early in the pregnancy.[17] This reason justified the Texas law that the Court invalidated in *Roe*. The antiabortion and protective life statutes struck down in *Roe* were justified, both because of the

---

[16] Foote, Levy, and Sander, *Cases and Materials on Family Law*, 2nd ed. (Boston: Little, Brown and Company, 1976), p. vii.

[17] Dr. and Mrs. J. C. Wilke, *Handbook on Abortion* (Cincinnati: Hayes Pub. Co., 1975), pp. 90–98 [hereafter referred to as *Handbook*].

states' interest in protecting pregnant women and in protecting unborn children.

3. *Women's rights.* The Supreme Court championed the rights of women to the point of extinguishing the fetus's right to live. Some women contend that the Court actually did women's rights a disservice in *Roe.* They contend that traditionally in America, women, and especially mothers, have enjoyed a position of great respect and high honor because of their partnership with God in bringing children into the world. While not content with everything in the traditional role of women in our society, they feel that many women have been overly militant in pressing for equal rights with men—so much so that the divine role of motherhood has been diminished and belittled. *Roe,* they say, is one sad example of the results of this overzealous advocacy.[18]

One woman has suggested that the *Roe* decision is an example of male chauvinism on the part of the Supreme Court Justices. Her reasoning is that the male chauvinism of the Justices leads them to be unduly protective of women at the expense of others; the men feel so sorry for the uncomfortable plight of the pregnant women that they go too far in attempting to protect them from discomfort.

C. Due Process Rights of the Fetus

The Court held that a fetus is not a "person" within the meaning of the Fourteenth Amendment and accordingly refused to recognize any due process rights for the fetus (410 U.S. 157). However, the

---

[18] Alexis de Tocqueville attributed the prosperity and strength of America to the superiority of its women, in that American women are esteemed to be of equal value with men but to have a different role in society. See Alexis de Tocqueville, *Democracy in America* (translated by Henry Reeve), vol. II, book 3, chapter XII (New York: Schocken Books, 1961), pp. 251–252, 254–255.

Court could have easily found such a right within the Constitution. The right to privacy is not explicitly enumerated in the Constitution, and yet the Court found it to exist within the penumbras of the First, Third, Fourth, Fifth, Ninth and Fourteenth Amendments (*Griswold v. Connecticut*, 381 U.S. 479 [1965]). It would be no more difficult to find the right to life for unborn children. The very basis of law in America is that men are "endowed by their Creator with certain unalienable rights," including the right to life (Declaration of Independence). In other words, rights come from God.[19]

1. *The Ninth Amendment.* The Ninth Amendment was designed to protect all basic rights of people that are not specifically enumerated in the Constitution: "The enumeration in the Constitution, of certain rights, shall not be construed to deny or disparage others retained by the people." Alexander Hamilton and others insisted on this amendment so that the government could not transgress any rights that did not happen to be enumerated in the Constitution. Yet, in *Roe*, the Court completely ignored this amendment and did exactly what our founding fathers sought to prohibit—that is, they said that because fetal rights are not specifically enumerated in the Constitution, the state cannot recognize such rights.[20]

---

[19] The Declaration of Independence was to set forth the moral justification of a rebellion against a long-recognized tradition—the divine right of kings. At issue was the fundamental question of whether men's rights were God-given or whether these rights were to be dispensed by governments to their subjects. This document proclaimed that all men have certain inalienable rights. In other words, these rights came from God. Therefore, the colonists were not rebels against political authority but free people only exercising their rights before an offending, usurping power. They were morally justified to do what they did. (Ezra Taft Benson, Conference Address, *Ensign*, November 1976, p. 33.)

[20] The Constitution does not specify how unenumerated rights were to be identified. Identifying them through a constitutional amendment is undoubtedly one proper way. Another way would be to identify them through state legislation in accordance with the Tenth Amendment. A more questionable method would be to identify such rights through implication (the court inferring that the Constitution implies their existence). The sad irony in *Roe* is that the Court identified the unenumerated woman's right to an abortion

As has already been mentioned, the Court used the Ninth Amendment to find the right to privacy and yet felt justified in not even checking to see whether the fetal right to life could also be found therein.

The Court could have also found support for the fetal right to life in the preamble to the Constitution: "We the People of the United States, in order to ... secure the Blessings of Liberty to ourselves and our Posterity, do ordain and establish this CONSTITUTION for the United States of America." The fetal right to life is a constitutional imperative if we are to "secure the Blessings of Liberty to ... our Posterity."

Without the right to life, there can be no other rights. Mr. Justice Brennan said that the right to life is the "right to have rights."[21] Prior to *Roe*, the fetal right to life had been directly protected through antiabortion statutes throughout the country and indirectly through marriage requirements, antifornication and antiadultery statutes, property law, social security regulations, descent and distribution law, and tort law. If fetuses enjoy rights in these areas, then they must necessarily also enjoy the more fundamental right to live. The Court, however, did not look at these other fetal rights in this manner. Instead it emphasized that all of these rights are contingent upon live birth and that fetuses have never been recognized as a "person" in the whole sense (410 U.S. 162). Neither of these reasons support a conclusion that the fetus does not have a right to life. The fact that a fetus is not a whole person in every respect that born children are persons does not mean that a fetus cannot have the right to life. And the fact that fetal rights are contingent does not mean that a fetus cannot have a right to life. Contingent rights are still rights, and obviously the contingency was never intended to be used to extinguish those rights by killing their owner.

---

by bare implication yet denied the existence of the unenumerated fetal right to life, which was explicitly protected in accordance with the Tenth Amendment.

[21] *Furman v. Georgia*, 408 U.S. 238, 272 (1968) (Brennan, J., concurring) (death penalty case).

Another flaw in the Court's reasoning is its presumption that by recognizing a fetal right to life, it would also have to afford *all* rights of born human beings to fetuses. This conclusion is also illogical. Fetuses need not be given the full rights of citizens in order to have the right to life. For example, there is no reason to give a fetus the right to drive or to vote.

The fact that most fetal rights are now contingent upon subsequent birth should have made it easy for the Court to find the fetal right to life. The Court should have found, as mentioned above, that if fetuses enjoy these other rights, they necessarily must also enjoy the right to life in order to protect their contingent rights. The Court should have construed the contingency to be a condition that cannot be manipulated to extinguish any potential fetal rights or to extinguish the fundamental right to life.

Some authorities feel reluctant to use the Ninth Amendment to materialize unenumerated rights because of its breadth. It is felt to be so broad that it is empty. Prior to the 1965 *Griswold* case, the Supreme Court only rarely referred to it at all.[22] However, to ignore it is to make it of no effect. Obviously it was intended to have some effect. When conflicts arose that could be solved by either referring to the due process clauses of the Fifth and Fourteenth Amendments *or* by the Ninth Amendment, lawyers and judges alike have almost exclusively opted to use the due process clause because it is felt to be more meaningful in light of the common law. Even when the Court has endorsed the existence of various "natural law" rights (rights that everyone just knows exist but that are not enumerated explicitly in the Constitution), it has used the due process clauses rather than the Ninth Amendment. However, all this tradition does not erase the amendment.

It has been argued additionally that the Ninth Amendment was intended to retain for the people only those rights that were protected

---

[22] 381 U.S. 479, 490–491, n. 6 (1965) (Goldberg, J., Warren, C. J., and Brennan, J., concurring, note 1).

under the English common law. Thus, it is said that because the fetal right to life was not recognized under the common law, the Ninth Amendment cannot be used to establish such a right. This interpretation, however, conflicts with the plain meaning of the amendment. The Ninth Amendment does not say that a right must be enumerated somewhere or recognized somewhere before the Constitution was written in order to be retained by the people. The Declaration of Independence makes it clear that rights come from God. The fact that no law in the eighteenth century explicitly protected the fetal right to life does not forever foreclose it from recognition under the Ninth Amendment.

(a) *Fetal rights in criminal law.* In criminal law, the fact that fetal rights are not contingent is sufficient for establishing the fetal right to life. The Court, however, did not address this contention, except in the historical context of how the laws have changed throughout the years. But the very fact that abortion was made a crime in almost every state for more than a hundred years (until 1967) indicates that it was the prevailing belief that a fetal right to life existed. Pro-abortionists attempt to denigrate this fact by emphasizing that such laws were for the protection of the mother. This is only part of the truth. No criminal law would be necessary to merely protect the mother. Women are not forced to have abortions. Many other elective operations were far more dangerous than abortion, yet no other such operations were made crimes.[23] Obviously, the criminal, antiabortion laws were intended to protect fetal life.[24] The Court's failure to address this contention is a basic flaw in the *Roe* decision.

(b) *Fetal rights in civil law.* In "areas other than criminal abortion," the Court stated that the law has been reluctant to enforce fetal rights except those contingent upon live birth (410 U.S. at 161).

---

[23] *Handbook*, pp. 156–157.

[24] William R. Hopkin Jr., "Roe v. Wade and the Traditional Legal Standards Concerning Pregnancy," *Temple Law Quarterly* 47 (1973–74): 715, 724–725.

This conclusion is not entirely accurate. Many states enforced fetal rights in certain instances regardless of whether the fetus was born alive.[25] One researcher said:

> [W]here a child dies as a result of prenatal injuries, the majority of courts will entertain an action for wrongful death without requiring the fetus to have been viable when injured. The majority of courts do not even require that the child be born alive. (William R. Hopkin Jr., "Roe v. Wade and the Traditional Legal Standards Concerning Pregnancy," *Temple Law Quarterly* 47 [1973–74]: 715, 724)

In areas other than the criminal law, fetal rights have been so widely recognized that the fetal right to life was obviously implicitly protected. The fact that fetal rights were often contingent upon live birth does not support the conclusion that the fetus has no right to life. Certainly these contingencies were not intended to denigrate the fetus's right to continue living so as to later enjoy the contingent right. The contingency is appropriate in many instances because the fetus is not capable of directly benefiting from such rights until its live birth. Our law is filled with contingencies relating to age and capacity. Driver's license requirements are one obvious example. It would be absurd to say that because a child's right to drive is contingent upon certain requirements that the child does not have a right to live. It is no less absurd to apply this reasoning to fetuses.

---

[25] Seventeen states and the District of Columbia have allowed stillborn babies to recover for injuries suffered as viable fetuses: Connecticut, Delaware, District of Columbia, Georgia, Indiana, Kansas, Kentucky, Louisiana, Maryland, Michigan, Minnesota, Mississippi, Nevada, New Hampshire, Ohio, South Carolina, West Virginia, and Wisconsin. Fifteen states do not allow stillborn babies to recover for prenatal injuries: Alabama, California, Florida, Illinois, Iowa, Massachusetts, Missouri, Nebraska, New Jersey, New York, North Carolina, Oklahoma, Pennsylvania, Tennessee, and Virginia. Hopkin, supra, note 44, at 721–722.

(c) *Right of inheritance.* Unborn children have had the right of inheritance since the eighteenth century in England.[26] In America, this fetal right is also recognized.[27]

(d) *Right to Social Security benefits.* In 1969, the US Court of Appeals for the Fifth Circuit held that a fetus had the right to receive Social Security benefits, the same as any other of a deceased father's children.[28]

(e) *Fetal right to life.* In 1964, a New Jersey court ordered blood transfusions to save the life of a pregnant woman and her unborn child, thereby recognizing the fetal right to life.[29]

(f) *Tort law rights.* In tort law, fetal rights became firmly recognized by the middle of the twentieth century. In 1884, Justice Oliver Wendell Holmes ruled that an unborn baby was "not a person" in the eyes of the law.[30] However, Professor Prosser says there has been a sweeping reversal of this legal principle (called the Dietrich doctrine). Practically every jurisdiction now holds that the fetus has a right to sue for injuries prior to birth.[31] In *Allaire v. St. Luke's Hospital,* 184 Ill. 359, 56 N.E. 638 (1900), a fetus was denied recovery for injuries, but the dissent written by Justice Boggs in that case soon became the majority view in almost every court—the view that viable fetuses can recover for prenatal injuries if subsequently born alive.[32] The case

---

[26] *Doe v. Clark,* 2H. Bl. 399, 126 Eng. Rep. 617; *Thelluson v. Woodford,* 4 Ves. 277, 31 Eng. Rep. 117.

[27] See, e.g., *Swain v. Bowers,* 91 Ind. 307, 158 N.E. 598 (1927).

[28] *Wagner v. Gardner,* 413 F.2d 267 (1969).

[29] *Raleigh Fitkin-Paul Morgan Memorial Hospital v. Anderson,* 42 N.J. 421, 201 A.2d 537, cert. denied, 377 U.S. 985 (1964).

[30] *Dietrich v. Inhabitants of Northhampton,* 138 Mass. 14 (1884).

[31] W. Prosser, *Handbook of the Law of Torts* (4th ed. 1971) at 337, n. 31.

[32] Hopkin, *supra,* at 719. The pertinent portion of Justice Boggs's dissent is as follows: "The law should ... be that whenever a child *in utero* is so far advanced in prenatal age as that, should parturition by natural or artificial means occur at such age, such child could and

of *Bonbrest v. Kotz*, 65 F. Supp. 138 (D.D.C. 1946), is now regarded as the leading case on allowing recovery for prenatal injuries.[33] By the early 1950s, the viability contingency recommended by Justice Boggs was discarded as being irrelevant by most courts. Since then, the overwhelming trend has been to recognize the fetal right to recover for injuries regardless of the stage of gestation, provided the child is subsequently born alive.[34]

The Court in *Roe* gives the impression that the law generally did not recognize fetal rights.[35] This is not correct; to the contrary, a substantial body of law throughout the United States conflicted with the Court's conclusion. In commenting on the cases relied upon by the Court in the *Roe* opinion, Professor Ely noted: "To the extent that they are not entirely inconclusive, the bodies of doctrine to which the Court adverts respecting the protection of fetuses under general legal doctrine tend to undercut rather than support its conclusions."[36]

Hopkin fully agrees with Ely's conclusions:

> Specifically, where most states today would permit recovery for prenatal injuries regardless of the stage of gestation in which the injuries are inflicted, the Court stated that recovery is granted only where the fetus is viable, or at least quick. The two citations

---

would live separable from the mother and grow into the ordinary activities of life, and is afterwards born and becomes a living human being, such child has a right of action for any injuries wantonly or negligently inflicted upon his or her person at such age of viability, though then in the womb of the mother" (56 N.E. 638, 642).

[33] Prosser, *supra*, at 336. For a list of cases following *Bonbrest*, see Annot., 4 A.L.R.3e 1222, 1230 (1971).

[34] Hopkin, *supra*, at 720, notes 32 and 33.

[35] 410 U.S. 161–162.

[36] Ely, "The Wages of Crying Wolf: A Comment on Roe v. Wade," 82 *Yale L. J.* 920, 925 (1973).

given here by the Court do not support its position. One states the law to be the contrary, and the other has only limited applicability, in wrongful death cases. Furthermore, many commentators do not oppose the recent development permitting the parents of a stillborn child to maintain an action for wrongful death because of prenatal injuries. Of the two commentators cited by the Court, one neither supports nor opposes the trend, and the other supports the trend. Both state that the trend now represents the majority view, which it does.

In short, tort law affords the unborn child substantial recognition. Courts will award damages for prenatal injuries regardless of the state of gestation of the fetus when the injury occurred. Similarly, where a child dies as a result of prenatal injuries, the majority of courts will entertain an action for wrongful death without requiring the fetus to have been viable when injured. The majority of courts do not even require that the child be born alive. Only in one narrow area of tort law do courts today generally attach significance to viability and deny recovery— where the fetus is not viable when injured, and is subsequently stillborn.[37]

Thus, as has been shown, there existed an abundance of precedence that should have compelled the Supreme Court to find that the fetal right to life is a right retained by the people under the Ninth Amendment. The Court failed to find this right because it failed to consider the things mentioned above. The Court did not find the fetal right to life because it did not look for it.

1. *The American Medical Association.* The Court was undoubtedly

---

[37] Hopkin, *supra,* at 123–124.

influenced by the drastic change in position taken by the American Medical Association (AMA) between 1859 and 1970. In 1859, the AMA adopted resolutions protesting "against the unwarrantable destruction of human life."[38] In 1970, however, the AMA, in response to the mounting pressures for abortions and because of the diversity of opinions among their profession as to the propriety of abortion, adopted a more lenient policy permitting abortion.[39] Notably, though, they did not conclude that a fetus was no longer "human life." Rather, they emphasized the importance of considering the "interest of the patients [pregnant women]." Unfortunately, the Court did not see through the AMA's inconsistencies. The AMA changed its policy to permit doctors to perform abortions without retracting its conclusion that a fetus is "human life." Instead of noting this inconsistency (perhaps the Court did not notice it), the Court got carried away in advocating women's rights and stressed that abortions no longer present such a great threat to women. But as was mentioned earlier, antiabortion laws were passed to protect fetuses, not pregnant women.

Even if abortions are now safer for women than before,[40] the AMA does not deny that fetuses are alive. That abortions may now be safer for women does not mean that the fetal right to life no longer can exist. In response to mounting proabortion pressure, the AMA threw in the towel to allow doctors to do what they each choose to do rather than to maintain a responsible stand against the taking of all "human life." But the AMA's irresponsibility is no justification for the Court's attempt to absolve itself of the responsibility to protect human life. The Court irresponsibly adopted the AMA's pass the buck policy.

---

[38] AMA position statement quoted by the Court at 410 U.S. at 141.

[39] *Id.* At 143.

[40] Some experts refute the theory that abortions performed at an early stage are safer for pregnant women than childbirth. There remains some question as to the effect of having an abortion on the psychological and long-term physical health of the woman. *Handbook, supra,* 49-53 and 90-97.

There is some question as to whether the AMA represents the nation's doctors accurately anymore. A poll released on December 4, 1976, by the Louisiana State Medical Society indicated that 64.8 percent of two thousand responding doctors felt the AMA "was not representing their personal views." The AMA disputed the poll. UPI Press Release, Provo *Daily Herald*, December 7, 1976, p. 9.

It is unquestionably true that there is no uniform consensus of opinion among members of the AMA on abortion. Dr. Wilke said:

> To say that there is a consensus of opinion would be a wild exaggeration. There is a deep disagreement between members of the A.M.A. on the question of abortion. All that has been voted on approvingly by its House of Delegates is a rather carefully worded document which, in so many words, says that a doctor may do what the law says is legal. Whether this policy will continue or will be changed next year is anybody's guess. (*Handbook*, supra, 133–34)

While the Court in *Roe v. Wade* relied somewhat on the AMA's new, more lenient abortion policy as justification for not recognizing the fetal right to life, it may very well be that the AMA was merely establishing a policy more in line with some of the recent changes in certain state laws that recognized abortion to be a legitimate medical procedure in some instances. If this is what happened, it makes a perfect case of the blind leading the blind.

Dr. Wilke's analysis of doctors' views on abortion includes the following additional statements:

> **How have the doctors responded to this new [AMA] policy?**
>
> This tentative policy has been deeply divisive. Some physicians have resigned from the A.M.A. over this

issue but most have remained as members and are working toward re-establishing the policy of respect for life upon which medicine is founded.

It is not unreasonable to predict that if its official policy would permanently become pro-abortion, the A.M.A. would lose a significant segment of its membership. If this happens it would lose its effectiveness as a unified voice of American medicine, as other medical organizations of different philosophies would grow in size and influence.

What do medical schools teach?

Since the discovery of conception over 100 years ago and until about ten years ago, it was taught that human life began at conception, should be protected, and that the only abortion that was ethical was a "therapeutic abortion" to save the mother's life.

For the last decade, largely convinced that "woman must have this right" most medical schools have been justifying abortion on the grounds that "the fetus is not yet human."

You mean, doctors are not informed?

That is true. This is not necessarily a criticism of doctors who commonly are narrowly specialized. A brain surgeon doesn't know much fetology. A surgeon or an internist doesn't know much fetology. Unless the doctor actually treats or delivers babies or has studied the area he or she may know only what is remembered from medical school plus recent knowledge from Time Magazine, the Journal articles (above) and similar biased input from an occasional medical meeting, etc ....

It is, incidentally, the rare doctor who has actually done or witnessed an abortion especially a late one. We have commonly appalled most doctors in our audience when we have shown the short "suction abortion" movie (a clinical teaching film available from Cincinnati Right to Life.) [sic]

Those doctors closest to the problem, Neonatologists, are almost all firmly opposed to abortion. The specialty most in favor, Psychiatry, is the group furthest removed from obstetric and pediatric care. (*Handbook*, supra, 134–36)

In the early 1970s, in England only 4 percent of the gynecologists favored abortion on demand. Ninety-eight percent of the delegates of the German Medical Association voted against abortion on demand. In response to a proposal for legalized abortion in France, seventeen thousand of the fifty thousand practicing physicians signed a petition calling for the full protection of human life from conception. Only three hundred proabortion signatures were collected, almost one hundred of which were shown to be invalid (*Handbook*, *supra*, 136, 139).

2. *The failure to differentiate between biological and spiritual life.* The Court only compounded, confused, and jumbled things when it coupled this medical change in position with the theological uncertainty of when the spirit enters the body. The Court considered the two problems to be one; but such is not the case. Biologically and medically, there is no question that life exists from conception. This is not even a subject of debate,[41] except when confused with

---

[41] "After the second week following fertilization, there is rapid differentiation of certain organs—for example, brain, heart, liver; and by the end of six weeks the rudimentary development of all internal organs has normally taken place. It is common, from the

the question of when the life of the soul begins. The Court confused the two issues and accordingly said that it need not decide when life begins (410 U.S. at 159). In the 1850s and 1860s, when most of the criminal antiabortion statutes were passed, there was no need to decide the theological question of when the spirit "quickens" the body. It was felt that the right to preserve fetal life existed regardless of when this happens. In *Roe*, however, the Court used this uncertainty to dodge the fetal right-to-life issue. The Court apparently felt that by labeling fetal rights as a religious question that it could avoid the question altogether. Of course, this type of reasoning did not prevent the Court from adopting the religious philosophy that a fetus has no right to life. The Court only fooled itself if it thought it could decide *Roe* without adopting some religious philosophy as the law. The Court further confused itself by reasoning that it must decide when the spirit enters the fetus's body in order to decide when fetal life begins. While this is a religious question, it does not require an answer in order to decide the fetal right-to-life question.

One of the most remarkable things about the *Roe* decision is how quickly the Court jumped from uncertainty about when life begins

eighth week, to refer to this nascent life as a *fetus*. At this time fingers and toes are recognizable, the skeleton takes form, the fetus has developed eyes but no eye lids, and simple reflex actions can be observed. No new major structures will be added to the organism; the remainder of the gestation period (approximately thirty weeks) will be spent in growth and maturation."

"By the twelfth week bone and cartilage are clearly recognizable, the fetal heartbeat can be detected by electrocardiogram (EKG), and some movement may occur because of muscle and nerve development. The eyelids, nose, mouth, lips, ears, fingers, and toes are fully formed by the sixteenth week. If the fetus should for any reason spontaneously abort prior to the twentieth week, this natural expulsion is customarily called a miscarriage. After the twentieth week, such a natural expulsion of the fetus is referred to as premature birth. The period from the twentieth week to parturition (i.e., birth) is characterized by little change in the external appearance of the fetus, but internal organs (especially the brain, for example) undergo accelerated development. Viability of the fetus (i.e., its ability to live after birth) is ordinarily calculated from the beginning of the twenty-eighth week. And if all else goes well, some time around the 266th day since fertilization the zygote-trophoblast-embryo-fetus is delivered as a bouncing baby-boy-girl-infant-child." Harmon L. Smith, *Ethics and the New Medicine* [Nashville: Abingdon Press, 1970], p. 19.

to the conclusion that regardless of the answer to this question, the right to life does not begin until birth. The remainder of the Court's opinion is founded upon this blatant error in reasoning. This basic internal flaw in reasoning undermines almost the entire opinion.

(a) *Conception—a process over time.* The Court also attempted to justify its decision by saying that conception might be a process over time rather than a moment in time (410 U.S. 160–61). But even if it is a process over time, it does not follow that a fetus does not have a right to life once conception *is* complete and a new, independent life comes into existence. It is only logical that the right to life exists whenever life itself exists. Medical experts have established that independent life can be detected in a developing fetus after only a few weeks.[42] Biologically, independent life exists from the moment the sperm and egg form a human zygote. From that point on, nothing but nourishment will be added to the independent life. While there is some uncertainty as to when fertilization is complete, there is no reason why this or any unknowns should be presumed to mandate that the new life cannot have the right to live. Doubts as to the existence of life should be resolved in favor of life; otherwise one runs the risk of condoning, encouraging, or actually doing the killing of a human life. The Court, however, chose to arbitrarily and irrationally deprive all prenatal life of the right to continue living.

(b) *The fetus—an extension of the mother.* In all fairness to the Court, it did not fall for this outdated theory. Basic biological knowledge repudiates this.[43] Even elementary school children realize that independent life exists in fertilized animal eggs. Marsupials

---

[42] *Id.*

[43] John P. Wilson, with the Department of Health, Education, and Welfare, reported the following:

> Some older judicial opinions, e.g., *Dietrich v. Northampton*, go farther than *Roe v. Wade* and hold that fetuses are merely part of the woman bearing them and thus have no independent rights whatsoever. Under this theory, the woman enjoys unrestricted authority over the fetus.

provide an especially good analogy for the fetal right-to-life argument. Marsupial babies (kangaroos, for example) are born before they can live on their own. The mother secures them in her pouch until they grow and develop enough to survive outside the pouch. In humans, birth would not be the key event if human babies were born before they were viable as are marsupial babies. Just as marsupial babies are totally dependent upon their mothers before and after birth, so are human babies totally dependent upon others before and after their birth. Biologically, there is no question that independent life exists before birth. Just as the fetus is an independent life, so does it also possess independent, God-given rights, which are not an extension of the mother's rights.

But, unlike the woman's appendix, the fetus (as well as the placenta, amniotic sac, and umbilical cord) is composed of chromosomes from her male partner as well as herself. It therefore has a separate biological identity. The *Roe v. Wade* decision did not, by its terms, give the woman absolute control over the fetus. The Court held that the mother had a constitutional right to abort it, that is, to remove it from her body. Death may be the natural and usual consequence of abortion, but the Court did not explicitly grant the mother a right to terminate fetal existence, nor did the Court grant her any right to experiment with the fetus and possibly harm its future development.

It is therefore my opinion that there should be no difference in the rights accorded to a previable or viable fetus. If the mother intends to carry a fetus to full term, it should be protected against all but the most innocuous forms of non-therapeutic research, whatever its stage of development. If therapeutic research is required for either the mother or pre-viable fetus, the same weighing of interests should occur as in the case of the viable fetus. The mother's interests should prevail conclusively only when there would be substantial danger to her life or health.

John P. Wilson, "A Report on Legal Issues Involved in Research on the Fetus," *Appendix—Research on the Fetus*, The National Commission for the Protection of Human Subjects of Biomedical and Behavioral Research (HEW) (1976).

For additional comments by doctors regarding fetal experimentation, see the report *Fetal Research* (July 19, 1974) of the hearing before the Subcommittee on Health of the Committee on Labor and Public Welfare, US Senate, 93rd Congress (Sen. Edward Kennedy, chair).

(c) *A comparison of birth and death.* A comparison of birth and death should be very helpful in identifying when the fetal right to life should begin. Death is measured in the law in medical terms of when the heart stops beating or when the brain ceases to function. The theological question of when the spirit leaves the body is not crucial in determining when death occurs. The law is able to function without resolving when the spirit enters or leaves a body. In addition, deceased people retain certain rights as well as obligations after death even when there is no question that they are not alive either spiritually or physically.[44] Similarly, the human fetus could have rights *before* the spirit enters. The unresolved theological question need not prevent a fetus from having the right to life. Fetuses have a heartbeat and a functioning brain as early as after forty days.[45] The law should at least protect the fetal right to life from this point. Why need there be a double standard for death and birth?

In summary, there was ample legal precedent from which the Court could have determined that a fetus cannot be deprived of its life without due process of law. The Ninth Amendment clearly states that the fact that rights are not enumerated in the Constitution shall not be construed to disparage the existence of such rights retained by the people. The Tenth Amendment reserves to the states the right to recognize and protect such unenumerated rights as the fetal right to life. As has been shown, all states recognize that fetuses have rights. All states continue to protect fetal life through marriage laws. And most states specifically recognized and protected the fetal right to life through antiabortion statutes prior to *Roe*. The fetal right to life was obviously a right retained by the people and accordingly should have been recognized by the Court, rather than completely ignored.

---

[44] A decedent enjoys the right to dispose of his/her property in accordance with a will or a state's laws of intestate succession. A decedent retains many of the liabilities he/she incurred such that his/her estate pays them.

[45] See note 36, *supra*, and *Handbook*, p. 18.

3. *A right to abort is not a right to kill.* Even though in many abortions it is impossible to abort without killing the fetus, there are also some abortions where the fetus can survive abortion. And with advances in medical technologies, it will be possible for more and more fetuses to survive abortions. In the future, not only will viable fetuses be able to survive premature births and abortions, but it is foreseeable that even previable fetuses will also be able to survive abortions.

This concept was recognized by some people at the time *Roe v. Wade* was decided in 1973, but it is even more widely recognized today, almost fifty years later.

The dilemma of what to do with fetuses who survive abortions was recently in the national spotlight in January 2019 when Governor Ralph Northam of Virginia was recorded stating that a proposed Virginia law would provide that if a fetus was alive after an abortion that the "infant" would be "kept comfortable" until "a decision would ensue between the physician and the mother." (Governor Northam actually referred to the surviving fetus as an "infant" three times.)[46] The chilling, unspoken message was that they would decide whether to kill the surviving "infant." Such a discussion is horrific and barbaric. The premise of Gov. Northam's statement is a false one—that the right to abort a fetus equals the right to kill a fetus. But for all the flaws in the *Roe v. Wade* decision, the Court did not actually say that. A right to abort does not necessarily mean a right to kill. Thus, under *Roe v. Wade*—without overturning or even modifying *Roe v. Wade*—states have the right to provide for the protection of fetal life at the same time they accommodate whatever right to abortion a woman may have.

This issue also drew considerable national attention in 2008,

---

[46] Gov. Northam said: "The infant would be delivered. The infant would be kept comfortable. The infant would be resuscitated if that's what the mother and the family desired, and then a discussion would ensue between the physicians and the mother." Reported by Scott Jennings, *USA Today*, February 5, 2019.

when Illinois Senator Barack Obama was running for president. As an Illinois state senator, Barack Obama voted against a proposed Illinois law that would have given some protection to fetuses that survived late-term abortions. His position on this matter was reprehensible then, and it continues to be so now.

Whatever right to an abortion exists under *Roe v. Wade* can accommodate measures to preserve and protect potential human life. The Court in *Roe* specifically acknowledged and provided for such measures when it provided that in the last trimester (or upon the fetus becoming viable), the states can regulate abortion in order to protect the potential human life. Consequently, without the slightest modification of *Roe*, states and/or Congress can pass laws to protect potential human life, and thus, the right to an abortion established in *Roe* can be limited in order to also protect unborn babies. All of this can happen without overturning *Roe v. Wade*.

D. Whose Right to Life?

The Court in *Roe* did say that the state has a right to protect potential human life.[47] This allows each state to protect fetal life in the last trimester if it chooses, but it does not guarantee that fetuses will be protected, nor does it give fetuses any right to be protected. It is inconsistent for the Court to say that the state has a right to protect fetal life, while saying that the fetus itself has no right to live. It would seem that if the state has a right to protect fetal life, certainly the fetus must also possess that right.

---

[47] The Court never does admit that a human fetus is "human life." It clings to this ridiculous semantic distinction to justify not recognizing the fetal right to life. By saying that a fetus is not human life until birth, the Court can more easily conclude that no right to life exists. Nevertheless, a fetus is definitely alive before birth and is human if its parents are human.

E. No Rational Basis for Invalidating the Texas Law

Texas sought to protect the rights of the unborn by prohibiting abortions, except when the mother's health was at stake. In invalidating this law, the Court gave no explanation that the Texas law was either factually erroneous or unreasonable. Robert A. Destro made this astute analysis of some problems with the Court's reasoning in *Roe*:

> The Texas courts had determined that the unborn were human beings whose lives were deserving of legislative protection. The Supreme Court disagreed, holding that no state may override the rights of a pregnant woman by simply adopting "one theory of life" [410 U.S. at 162]. But the ultimate resolution of the question was not nearly as simple as the Court's language made it sound. Although the effect of the Court's holding was to forbid state protection of a class of individuals found to be human beings, the Court's opinion contains no finding that such a state determination would be either factually erroneous or so unreasonable as to be precluded by a broad interpretation of the Constitution.
>
> Since the Court was apparently unwilling to disclose the constitutional basis of this particular facet of its ultimate resolution of the merits of *Roe v. Wade*, the holding of necessity must rest upon a determination that the judicial power of the United States includes the right to restrict the protection

of fundamental liberties to those classes the Court deems worthy.[48]

As Justice Rehnquist said in his dissent in *Roe*: "The test traditionally applied in the area of social and economic legislation is whether or not a law such as that challenged has a rational relation to a valid state objective" (410 U.S. at 173). But the Court did not apply that test in *Roe*.

In a 1957 obscenity case, Justice Harlan said that "the very division of opinion on the subject counsels us to respect the choice made by the state."[49] In view of the uncertainty facing the Court in regards to fetal rights, the Court should have allowed the states to resolve these questions, in accordance with the Ninth and Tenth Amendments.

F. Viability

The Court in *Roe* established two conflicting standards for determining at what point a state could begin to protect fetal life: (1) beginning after twenty-four to twenty-eight weeks; and (2) when the fetus becomes able to survive outside the mother's womb (becomes viable). Neither of these standards is enforceable; one is too rigid, the other is too flexible.[50] No one would want to get hung up on a

---

[48] Robert A. Destro, "Abortion and the Constitution: The Need for a Life-Protective Amendment," *California L. Rev.* 63: 1250, 1259–1260 (1975).

[49] *Alberts v. California*, 354 U.S. 476, 502 (1957) (Harlan, J., concurring). This was the companion case to *Roth v. United States*, 354 U.S. 476 (1957).

[50] The Court made it clear three years later that the "viability" standard supersedes the strict, third trimester standard. *Planned Parenthood of Central Missouri v. Danforth*, 428 U.S. 52 (1976). Viability is "the stage of fetal development when the life ... may be continued indefinitely outside the womb by natural or artificial life-supportive systems" (428 U.S. at 63). Later, in *Webster v. Reproductive Services*, 492 U.S. 490, 519 (1989), the Court reaffirmed and reinforced "viability" as the point from which states can begin to protect fetal life.

difference of one or two days. But what about one or two weeks? There have been babies born after only twenty weeks who lived. Certainly those babies were viable. Twenty-four to twenty-eight weeks is only an average. Certainly averages are not meant to protect rights. If the Court intends to protect viable fetuses, the twenty-four to twenty-eight weeks' age requirement is inaccurate and unjust.

On the other hand, it is impossible to discern when a fetus becomes viable under the second standard. Too many unpredictable variables exist to make it enforceable, including (a) peculiarities of each individual woman, (b) peculiarities of each fetus, (c) differences in each pregnancy, and (d) the impossibility of determining when a fetus becomes capable of surviving outside of the womb. Had any other court or lawmaking body invented the viability distinction, the Supreme Court would have called it irrational, and they would have invalidated it. Perhaps the Supreme Court did as laudable a job as possible for humans to do in devising a viability distinction. But such a distinction is totally unnecessary. The only purpose this distinction serves is to divert attention from the fact that the Court now allows fetuses that are alive to be legally killed.

Some have postulated that the flexible viability distinction is a workable one that will remain valid in the future along with advances in technology:

> At some future time ... scientists may perfect a method whereby fetal life can be sustained outside the mother's womb from the moment of conception, in which case the state could prohibit all abortions. By focusing on compelling state interest rather than the traditional trimesters of pregnancy, *Roe* has achieved a flexibility which will allow it to survive in a world of rapidly changing medical technology. (Hopkin, *supra*, at 738)

There are, however, some problems with this view. First, this alleged virtue does not remedy the fact that it is still impossible to determine when viability begins. Only when technology will allow this determination to be accurately made can the flexible approach begin to be a workable standard. Second, this flexibility can work against fetal rights as well as for them. Third, it does not protect fetal life now. And fourth, even if such technological advances do come about, this still does not give fetuses a right to life; it only allows states to protect fetal life if they choose to do so.

The viability distinction is actually meaningless, as is demonstrated by the fact that no fetus can live either inside or outside of the mother's womb without help from someone. Generally, after twenty-four to twenty-eight weeks, a fetus has a chance to live outside of the mother's womb. But as a born baby, it will still be totally dependent upon others for its continued existence. The existence of life itself should determine whether the right to life exists, not whether a human has the ability to live on its own. Children are not capable of survival without help until they are *at least* three or four. There are many disabled people and invalids who cannot survive without help. It is ridiculous to equate the right to life with the right to "meaningful life," as the Court suggested in *Roe* (410 U.S. at 163). Such a standard is obviously as inapplicable to fetuses as it is to invalids. Actually, because the fetuses' potential for meaningful life is usually greater than that of many invalids, there is even greater reason to protect fetuses than to protect invalids.

In reality, the only change occurring at twenty-four to twenty-eight weeks is that at that point, other people acquire a responsibility to nourish and care for the baby in addition to the mother—that is, the father, the family, and the state. The Court should have recognized this rather than picking the point of viability to be when a state can begin to protect fetal life.[51]

---

[51] The question is, Does a fetus have any right to live at all? If a so-called viable fetus has a right to live, then so must all fetuses. The only difference between viable and nonviable fetuses is that the former are dependent upon the mother or someone else, while the latter

Until a fetus is viable, it is solely dependent upon its mother. Rather than using viability as the point when the state can begin to protect fetuses, this point should be designated as the time when the state, *in addition* to the mother, acquires a responsibility to nourish and protect the child. Certainly, the live fetus does not first acquire the right to live when he or she becomes viable. The right to life should be recognized as coexisting with life.

---

are dependent exclusively upon the mother. In one sense, all fetuses are viable—with help they can survive. Even when a fetus reaches the point where it could survive if born, it is still helplessly dependent upon others.

CHAPTER THREE

Proposed Constitutional Amendments

The right-to-life movement is not aimed at overturning *Roe*; it is aimed at protecting fetal life. Although the Court's decision in *Roe* accentuates the need for a constitutional amendment to specifically protect fetal life, such an amendment need not be characterized as merely an attempt to overrule that decision. Many constitutional scholars believe that because fetal rights were not specifically provided for in the Constitution, an amendment ought to be passed before the courts protect such rights.

The due process clauses of the Fifth and Fourteenth Amendments have historically ensured that a person is not deprived of life, liberty, or property without a procedurally fair determination that it would be just to do so. In recent years, the Supreme Court has come to enlarge the meaning of "due process" to include certain rights that do not involve procedures—that is, substantive rights.[52] The right to privacy is an example of such an unenumerated substantive right. While no

---

[52] In 1905, in the case of *Lochner v. New York*, 198 U.S. 45 (1905), the Supreme Court articulated the concept of "substantive due process" as a basis for recognizing rights that were not specifically mentioned in the Constitution.

one would deny that such a right should be protected, this right is not specifically enumerated in the Constitution, nor is it a procedural right. The Court correctly determined that this right is worthy of protection, but by recognizing this right, it took upon itself a lawmaking role. The Court said that the First, Third, Fourth, Fifth, Ninth, and Fourteenth Amendments implied the existence of this right.

While the Court's recognition of a right to privacy was laudable, *Roe* points out the inevitable result of allowing the Court to create rights: it creates rights it feels should be recognized and fails to recognize other rights that it feels are less worthy of recognition. The Court recognized a woman's right to have an abortion but denied that fetuses have a right to life.

Now that the Supreme Court has ruled there is no fetal right to life, it is up to Congress to re-establish that right, and that would be done through constitutional amendment. Certainly, no one can quarrel with the citizens' right to create new rights by passing a new amendment. If two-thirds of Congress and three-fourths of the states support such a law, then the ultimate sovereign—the people—will have spoken.

Amending the Constitution was undoubtedly one way in which the unenumerated Ninth Amendment rights were intended to be protected. Our Constitution has been aptly labeled a "living constitution."[53] The amending process is one of the highest expressions of this.

Originally, the Bill of Rights were held not to restrict states at all—only to restrict the federal government. Had John Marshall, one of the first chief justices of the Supreme Court, decided *Roe v. Wade* according to his reasoning in *Barron v. Baltimore*, 7 Pet. 243 (1833), the Supreme Court would not have invalidated the Texas law that prohibited abortion.

Now, however, almost all of the rights identified in the first Ten Amendments have been held to apply to the states through the

---

[53] Saul K. Padover, *The Living U. S. Constitution* (New York: Mentor Books, 1963).

Fourteenth Amendment. This process has been called "selective incorporation," and it has unfolded over a period of more than a hundred years. The latest right identified in the Bill of Rights that has been recently held by the Supreme Court to be binding upon the states is the right to bear arms (Second Amendment). In the cases of *District of Columbia v. Heller*, 554 U.S. 570 (2008) and *McDonald v. Chicago*, 561 U.S. 742 (2010), the Supreme Court held that states must recognize and protect an individual's right to bear arms. *Roe* represents a further expansion of the Bill of Rights. Some of this is good, but some is not. That expansion that prohibits states from protecting human life before birth is not good.

Under our constitutional system of checks and balances, there are two ways in which an erroneous or undesirable Supreme Court decision can be overruled: (1) the Court itself could reverse its prior decision, or (2) Congress can enact legislation (including proposing a constitutional amendment) to overrule the Court. Historically, the Court has been reluctant to reverse itself, although recently, activist justices on the Court reversed some of its recent rulings with respect to gay rights and same-sex marriage.[54] The best way to correct mistakes by the Supreme Court is through congressional legislation, but it is typically difficult to obtain the supermajority support required to enact a new amendment to the Constitution.

To establish a fetal right to life, a constitutional amendment is needed to explicitly enumerate this right. For such an amendment to become effective, two-thirds of both houses of Congress must vote for it, and three-fourths of the fifty state legislatures must vote to accept it by a majority vote.[55] As arduous a task as this may be, there is now no other way to restore the fetal right to life. Only through an increased awareness on the part of the public will the present state of

---

[54] See, for example, *United States v. Windsor, Lawrence v. Texas,* and *Obergefell v. Hodges,* and the discussion about them in chapter 6.

[55] United States Constitution, Article V.

the law be improved. With the help of a strong public outcry against the unwarranted taking of fetal life, this effort can succeed.

Some people feel that once the Supreme Court has spoken, the matter is ended. Sometimes it is. Regarding the Supreme Court decision on prayer in public schools, President Kennedy said, "I think that it is important for us, if we are going to maintain our constitutional principles, that we support the Supreme Court decisions, even though we may not agree with them."[56] This does not mean, however, that we should not attempt to change the law through the appropriate constitutional channels. Presidents Abraham Lincoln, Andrew Jackson, Thomas Jefferson, and Franklin D. Roosevelt have all addressed this issue and explained that under the separation of powers in our government, it was intended that executive and legislative branches act independently to uphold the Constitution and if necessary reverse the judicial branch through appropriate constitutional channels.[57]

---

[56] "Constitutional Aspects of the Right to Limit Childbearing," U. S. Commission on Civil Rights, Washington, DC, April 1975, p. 79.

[57] Abraham Lincoln said that supporting a Supreme Court decision does not prevent one from attempting to overturn that decision by changing the law. During the famous Lincoln-Douglas debates, Lincoln said the following:

> I have expressed heretofore, and I now repeat, my opposition to the Dred Scott Decision [*Dred Scott v. Sandford*, 19 How. 393 (1857)] .... I am opposed to [the Dred Scott] decision in a certain way, but not in the sense which [Douglas] puts on it. I say that in so far as it decided in favor of Dred Scott's master and against Dred Scott and his family, I do not propose to disturb or resist the decision ....
>
> We oppose the Dred Scott decision in a certain way, upon which I ought perhaps to address you a few words. We do not propose that when Dred Scott has been decided to be a slave by the court, we, as a mob will decide him to be free. We do not propose that, when any other one, or one thousand, shall be decided by that court to be slaves, we will in any violent way disturb the rights of property thus settled; but we nevertheless do oppose that decision as a political rule which shall be binding on the voter to vote for nobody who thinks it wrong, which shall be binding on the members of Congress or the President to favor no measure that does not actually concur with the principles of that decision. We do not propose to be bound by it as a political

President Lincoln said: "Bad laws, if they exist, should be repealed as soon as possible.[58] Lincoln espoused this principle in dealing with the Supreme Court's decision in *Dred Scott v. Sandford*, 19 How. 393 (1857). In that case the Court held that black people were not "persons" within the meaning of the Constitution. Eleven years later, Congress eventually passed the Thirteenth and Fourteenth Amendments to correct this problem. One cannot help but recognize the similarity between the *Dred Scott* and the *Roe* decisions. In both cases a class of human individuals were denied certain rights because the Court said they were not legal persons.

Three types of Amendments have been proposed to change the law regarding the fetal right to life: (1) That which reserves to each state the opportunity to establish this right if it desires to do so (S. J. Res. 143, at pages 44-45); (2) That which provides that fetuses are "persons" within the meaning of the Fourteenth Amendment (S. J. Res. 178, at pages 46-47); and (3) That which merely bestows on human fetuses the right to life[59] (H. J. Res. 41, at pages 48-49).

---

rule in that way, because we feel it lays the foundation not merely of enlarging and spreading that evil into the States themselves. We propose so resisting it as to have it reversed if we can. *(II Collected Works of Abraham Lincoln* [Basler, ed., 1953], pp. 494, 516; III id., 255)

Andrew Jackson said this: "The opinion of the judges has no more authority over Congress than the opinion of Congress has over the judges, and on that point the President is independent of both. The authority of the Supreme Court must not, therefore, be permitted to control the Congress or the Executive" when acting in their independent capacities. Veto Message (on bill to recharter the Bank of the United States), July 10, 1832 (II *Messages and Papers of the Presidents* (Richardson, ed. 1896), 576, 581–583.

Thomas Jefferson wrote the following to Abigail Adams on Sept. 11, 1804: "[T]he opinion which gives to the judges the right to decide what laws are constitutional and what not, not only for themselves in their own sphere of action, but for the Legislature & Executive also, in their spheres, would make the judiciary a despotic branch." *VIII The Writings of Thomas Jefferson* (Ford, ed. 1897), p. 310.

[58] Quoted by N. Eldon Tanner, *Conference Report*, October, 1965, pp. 46–49.

[59] Examples of each of these proposed amendments are shown at pages 41–49.
A semantical problem exists regarding the meaning of "human life." Some hold to the view that a fetus does not become "human life" until it reaches a certain stage in its

The states' rights proposal has some appeal because it allows each state to decide for itself whether or not to recognize the fetal right to life. However, such an amendment would prove to be ineffective even in those states that would choose to protect fetal life because women would merely travel to an abortion state to get a legal abortion.

Both of the latter proposals would establish the fetal right to life on a nationwide basis. Both proposals mention that a fetus is to be considered a "person." This leads to the question of whether the fetus's right to life is equal to a born person's right to life. I have not seen a proposed amendment that clarifies this question. Perhaps it is not necessary to describe the magnitude of the right to life in the amendment; perhaps the courts can draw these lines in the future.

This writer supports the second or third type of proposed amendment (S. J. Res. 178 or H. J. Res. 41 [94th Congress]). Neither proposal requires giving fetuses every right that born persons have. And neither proposal solves the problem of describing the exact magnitude of the fetal right. But drawing such lines can be done through the balancing in due process. In the past, the Court's problem was that it could find no fetal right to life. These proposals also provide that Congress shall have power to enforce this right by legislation, thus reserving to Congress, as well as to the Supreme Court, the duty of defining the scope of the fetal right to life. There is nothing objectionable in this.

Notably lacking among the arguments against a right-to-life amendment is the argument that fetuses do not have a right to live. Almost every argument against these proposals focuses on some imagined problem that would result if the fetal right to life becomes a recognized right. These arguments avoid the most fundamental issue of all: whether a human fetus has a right to live. If it does, no other issue is important enough to require that the right to life be denied altogether.

---

development, such as viability or birth. Undue concern about this semantic problem only confuses the real issue. A human fetus is not any different because of what it is called.

94TH CONGRESS
1ST SESSION **S. J. RES. 143**

IN THE SENATE OF THE UNITED STATES

OCTOBER 29, 1975

Mr. BURDICK introduced the following joint resolution; which was read twice
and referred to the Committee on the Judiciary

JOINT RESOLUTION

An amendment to the Constitution of the United States to give
the several States power to protect unborn children and
other persons.

1   *Resolved by the Senate and House of Representatives of*

2   *the United States of America in Congress assembled (two-*

3   *thirds of each House concurring therein),* That the follow-

4   ing article is proposed as an amendment to the Constitution

5   of the United States, which shall be valid to all intents and

6   purposes as part of the Constitution when ratified by the

7   legislatures of three-fourths of the several States within

8   seven years from the date of its submission by the Congress:

II

2

1   "ARTICLE —

2   "The Congress within Federal jurisdictions and the

3 several States within their respective jurisdictions shall have

4 power to protect life, including the unborn, at every state of

5 biological development irrespective of age, health, or con-

6 dition of physical dependency.".

94TH CONGRESS
1ST SESSION
S. J. RES. 143

JOINT RESOLUTION

An amendment to the Constitution of the
United States to give the several States
power to protect unborn children and other
persons.

By Mr. BURDICK

OCTOBER 29, 1975
Read twice and referred to the Committee on the
Judiciary

Calendar No. 666

94TH CONGRESS
2D SESSION # S. J. RES. 178 *

IN THE SENATE OF THE UNITED STATES

MARCH 15, 1976

Mr. HELMS introduced the following joint resolution; which was read twice
and ordered to be placed on the calendar

JOINT RESOLUTION

Proposing an amendment to the Constitution of the United States
guaranteeing the right of life to the unborn.

1   *Resolved by the Senate and House of Representatives of*

2   *the United States of America in Congress assembled (two-*

3   *thirds of each House concurring therein),* That the follow-

4   ing article is proposed as an amendment to the Constitution

5   of the United States, which shall be valid to all intents and

6   purposes as a part of the Constitution only if ratified by the

7   legislatures of three-fourths of the several States within seven

8   years from the date of its submission by the Congress:

9   "ARTICLE —

10   "SECTION 1. With respect to the right to life guaranteed

11   in this Constitution, every human being, subject to the juris-

---

*Identical to S. J. Res. 6 (94th Congress).

- 46 -

THE FETAL RIGHT TO LIFE ARGUMENT

1 diction of the United States, or of any State, shall be deemed,

2 from the moment of fertilization, to be a person and entitled

3 to the right to life.

4   "SEC. 2. Congress and the several States shall have

5 concurrent power to enforce this article by appropriate leg-

6 islation.".

Calendar No. 666

94TH CONGRESS
2D SESSION
S. J. RES. 178

JOINT RESOLUTION

Proposing an amendment to the Constitution of
the United States guaranteeing the right of
life to the unborn.

By Mr. HELMS

MARCH 15, 1976
Read twice and ordered to be placed on the calendar

94TH CONGRESS
1ST SESSION

H. J. RES. 41

IN THE HOUSE OF REPRESENTATIVES

JANUARY 14, 1975

Mr. DELANEY introduced the following joint resolution; which was referred to the Committee on the Judiciary

JOINT RESOLUTION

Proposing an amendment to the Constitution of the United States to insure that due process and equal protection are afforded to an individual from the moment of conception.

1 *Resolved by the Senate and House of Representatives of*
2 *the United States of America in Congress assembled (two-*
3 *thirds of each House concurring therein)*, That the following
4 article is proposed as an amendment to the Constitution of
5 the United States, which shall be valid to all intents and
6 purposes as part of the Constitution only if ratified by the
7 legislatures of three-fourths of the several States within
8 seven years from the date of its submission to the States
9 by Congress:

I

2

1   "ARTICLE —

2   "SECTION 1. No person, from the moment of concep-
3 tion, shall be deprived of life, liberty, or property without
4 due process of law; nor shall any person, from the moment
5 of conception, be denied equal protection of the laws.

6   "SEC. 2. Neither the United States nor any State shall
7 deprive any human being of life on account of age, illness,
8 or incapacity.

9   "SEC. 3. Congress and the several States shall have
10 power to enforce this article by appropriate legislation."

CHAPTER FOUR

The Disgraceful U. S. Commission on Civil Rights

You might think that the U. S. Commission on Civil Rights (hereafter "Commission") in 1975 would be able to make a thorough and objective analysis and report to Congress about all aspects of civil rights pertaining to proposed right-to-life amendments. But you would be wrong. In 1975, the Commission issued a report titled "Constitutional Aspects of the Right to Limit Childbearing," Washington, DC, April 1975 (hereafter referred to as "Report"). This Commission, established by Congress, recommended not passing any of the three types of proposed amendments. The Report is very one-sided; it reads as you would expect a lobbyist's brief in support of the woman's right to an abortion. It is extremely disappointing that our nation's Civil Rights Commission should be comprised exclusively of proabortion advocates who were unable to give a fair and objective analysis of the point of view of half of the nation that was supportive of recognizing a fetal right to life.

The purpose of this chapter is to present the substantial facts and arguments that the Commission ignored. The Commission did not even acknowledge most of these issues. The bias and the omissions of the Commission were so great that it was disgraceful. The Report represents second-rate scholarship. This chapter is in large measure intended to respond to the Report of the Civil Rights Commission and to point out its overt biases and its many flaws.

A. The First Amendment— Separation of Church and State

Finding number four of the Commission states:

> The proposed constitutional amendments are inconsistent with the history and law of the First Amendment in that they would give governmental sanction to one set of moral and religious views and inhibit the free exercise of any other moral and religious views on the issue of when life begins. (Report, p. 99)

This conclusion is ridiculous. Nothing in those proposed amendments is inconsistent with the First Amendment. Almost every law gives governmental sanction to somebody's moral or religious views *and* prohibits conduct that some may claim is permissible in their religion. However, no one is yet saying that their religion compels them to have an abortion. And even if this claim were made, the "free exercise" right in the First Amendment is not an absolute; conduct does not become immune from regulation merely because someone claims the religious right to engage in such conduct.[60]

The lack of logical reasoning in this finding by the Commission is further demonstrated by pointing out that the present state of the

---

[60] See, for example, *Reynolds v. United States*, 98 U.S. 145 (1878) (polygamy); *Jacobson v. Massachusetts*, 197 U.S. 11 (1905) (compulsory vaccination); and *Memorial Hospital v. Anderson*, 42 N.J. 421, cert. denied, 377 U.S. 958 (1964) (compulsory blood transfusion).

law fosters the religious view that the fetus does not have a right to live. The Commission's finding has an inherent inconsistency in that it inhibits the fetus's free exercise of religion. The Commission apparently did not realize that its conclusion cuts both ways.

1.   *Freedom of conscience.* The Commission reasoned that adopting a right-to-life amendment would be "a direct assault on the freedom of conscience" and would violate a woman's freedom of religion by establishing one religious view as the law. This is nonsense. A right-to-life amendment does not interfere in the least bit with an individual's right to believe what he or she will on abortion. A right-to-life amendment would regulate conduct. As was mentioned in the preceding two paragraphs, every law endorses somebody's moral view. The question is, Whose view? And in a democracy, it is the moral views of the majority that is the law.

2.   *When life begins.* The Commission also erred in concluding that a right-to-life amendment would establish one view on when life begins. They undoubtedly are referring to a legal concept of life, because there is no question biologically and medically that from conception an independent life exists in the mother's womb. The legal question of when life begins has nothing to do with the theological uncertainty of when the spiritual life of the fetus begins. Neither is the legal protection of fetuses dependent upon the resolution of whether theologically a spirit has a right to have its future fetal body protected. The legal question of when the right to life begins is not dependent upon any theological opinion of when the spirit enters the fetus or otherwise acquires a right therein. By recognizing the fetal right to life, no one is compelled to believe any particular theological doctrine.

3.   *A majority of voters establish rights.* The American nation was founded based upon the belief that an omnipotent Creator endowed every individual with certain unalienable rights. Freedom of belief and the separation of church and state, as embodied in the First Amendment, was never meant to prohibit individuals from forming

their political opinions based upon religious beliefs. If a majority of citizens hold the same political belief, regardless of whether or not it is based upon the same religious belief, then that viewpoint may properly be made the law. The First Amendment was not enacted to discourage religion but rather to protect small religions and to prevent any one religion from directly controlling the government.

B. The Ninth Amendment— Unenumerated Rights

Finding number five of the Commission states:

> The proposed constitutional amendments are inconsistent with the Ninth Amendment in that they would outlaw a common liberty held by American women when the Bill of Rights was adopted, as a right retained by the people which could not be disparaged or denied by the government. (Report, p. 99)

This is an absurd and erroneous argument. It is completely irrelevant in regards to amending the Constitution. The Ninth Amendment was not intended to prevent any further amendment of the Constitution. If anything, the Ninth Amendment mandates additional amendments in order to protect unenumerated rights.

The Commission is accurate in pointing out that a right-to-life amendment would, in many cases, interfere with a woman's right to have an abortion. Of course it would. That is the very purpose for passing a right-to-life amendment. And the fact that the Court for the first time in *Roe* found that a woman's right to have an abortion is partly implied by the Ninth Amendment is the very reason why a right-to-life amendment is necessary. The Court failed to recognize and balance the fetal right to life with the woman's right to have an abortion. So now an amendment is necessary in order to force the Court to recognize and consider the fetal right to life as well as the woman's right to privacy.

Another fallacy in the Commission's finding is that the Commission says that the Ninth Amendment "retains" for the people only those rights that were enumerated somewhere outside the Constitution. But this is not what the amendment says. The Ninth Amendment does not depend upon whether or not an unenumerated right was enumerated somewhere outside of the Constitution.

1.   *The common law right to an abortion.* The Commission argued that:

> To understand what rights were retained by the people one must look to the common and statute law in 1791. The freedom of a woman to abort was one right recognized under common law. (Report, p. 45)[61]

This finding is not determinative of whether a right is or is not retained by the people. The existence of rights under the Ninth Amendment is not contingent upon the existence of such rights in the common and statute law of England. While it may be proper to look to the 1791 English common law for historical purposes, such a search is conclusive neither for nor against a finding that a particular right is retained by the people. The Constitution was not created to be contingent upon any other law—not the English common law, nor English statutes, nor the Articles of Confederation, nor anything else. The very reason for establishing the United States Constitution was because the English laws were inadequate and contained too many flaws.

Under the English common law, abortions after quickening had occurred were illegal. In 1803, England enacted its first criminal

---

[61] Postquickening abortions were prohibited under the common law (410 U.S. 113, 132–136).

abortion statute, which made all abortions illegal.[62] Similarly, at a very early date in American history, the states enacted criminal abortion laws. This began in the 1820s and 1830s.[63] By 1867, at least thirty of the thirty-seven states had antiabortion statutes.[64]

2. *Were antiabortion laws enacted to protect women?* It is argued by some that state criminal abortion laws were enacted to protect women from the medical risks of having an abortion. Frankly, this is a misrepresentation. But the proponents of these arguments further argue that with the advancement of medical technology, the reason for antiabortion laws has disappeared. But that is absolutely false. These antiabortion laws were not enacted to protect women; they were enacted to protect fetal life.

In response to mounting evidence and advances in medical technology that positively demonstrated that independent life exists from conception, the American Medical Association, in 1859, passed a resolution calling for states to revise existing abortion laws to protect the fetal right to life from conception. Thereafter, for more than a hundred years, most states (if not all states) did have such laws. Prior to the 1800s, there was a lack of evidence to prove when independent biological life first existed. Quickening—when the mother first felt life—was considered the dividing point between when abortion would be permissible because it was not known whether there was a life in the mother until that point. However, when it was proven that independent human life existed from the time of conception, almost every state expanded their abortion laws to prohibit all abortions. When the Fourteenth Amendment was enacted in 1868, at least thirty of the thirty-seven states had laws prohibiting abortion.

---

[62] 410 U.S. at 136.

[63] Report, p. 46.

[64] 410 U.S. 113, 175–176. At least twenty-one of these statutes were still in effect in 1970.

Fetuses have independent biological life from conception, regardless of whether spiritual life is present. It is this biological life that the antiabortion statutes protect.[65] There is no need to deny the fetus of this right to life because of unresolved theological questions. Antiabortion statutes were never intended to be based upon one theological opinion or another; they were based upon evidence that biological life exists from conception.

It is true that abortion has now been made safer for women, but this does not change the fact that biological life exists from conception. Antiabortion statutes were enacted to protect fetuses, not women. The fact that abortion is now safer for women is irrelevant to whether the fetal right to life continues to exist.

C. The Fourteenth Amendment

A woman's due process rights—compulsory childbearing. The Commission argues that the proposed constitutional amendments would compel a woman to carry a child to delivery, regardless of whether or not she consented to intercourse or pregnancy.[66] It is argued that this would deprive her of her right not to be pregnant *without due process of the law* and require her to be pregnant and to assume the responsibilities of parenthood. The Commission also said:

> The amendments admit of no exceptions when a woman takes ineffective birth control pills or when a man uses a defective condom. There is no exception

---

[65] See, for example, *Kelley v. Gregory*, 282 App. Div. 542, 543-544, 125 N.Y.S.2d 696, 697 (N.Y. Sup. Ct. 1953): "We ought to be safe in this respect in saying that legal separability should begin where there is biological separability. We know something more of the actual process of conception and foetal [British spelling] development now than when some of the common law cases were decided; and what we know makes it possible to demonstrate clearly that separability begins at conception."

[66] Some view the prohibition of abortion as a punishment for fornication (405 U.S. 443, 448).

for duress or submitting to intercourse during marriage in order to avoid denial of consortium[67] as grounds for divorce. (Report, p. 62)

1. *Unwanted pregnancies.* To begin with, in this argument, the Commission seeks to separate the right to have intercourse from the consequences of pregnancy. The Commission is saying that there exists a right to participate in sexual intercourse *and* a right not to be pregnant even if a child is conceived from a voluntary act of intercourse. The law had never recognized that the right not to be pregnant extended that far, until *Roe.* On the contrary, our laws have made marriage a prerequisite to intercourse in order to ensure that parents assume the responsibility for the consequences of their sexual relations.

(a) *Contraceptive failure.* As to the situations where pregnancy is not wanted but where intercourse is willingly engaged in, the argument that the pregnancy was involuntary is neither logical nor valid. Any intelligent person knows that contraceptives are not 100 percent effective. There is always a chance that pregnancy may result from intercourse. Couples should be required to recognize that chance and responsibly accept the consequences that may result from their voluntary acts. If a woman voluntarily engaged in sexual intercourse, she has no basis for saying that her due process rights would be violated by making it illegal for her to abort the life she initiated through her own voluntary acts.

(b) *Compulsory childbearing.* The Commission further confuses things by the use of the word "compel." A woman is free to completely avoid childbearing by abstaining from intercourse. She is not compelled to have intercourse. Therefore, only in cases of rape or incest is the Commission's point about compelled childbearing

---

[67] In the 1970s, refusal to participate in sexual intercourse with a spouse for over an eighteen-month period constituted grounds for divorce in some places. Such a denial of sexual intercourse could be a "denial of consortium."

relevant at all. By making unwarranted abortions illegal, a woman is not "compelled" to bear children. She can always choose not to engage in sexual intercourse. And if she takes the risk and becomes pregnant, yes, she has a responsibility to care for the life she partnered in creating. If she chooses to have an illegal abortion, then she may have to pay a penalty for this decision. But the law does not compel her to obey.

(c) *Rape and incest.* In cases where pregnancy was forced upon a woman through rape or incest, there does exist a good argument that a woman should not be forced to be pregnant and to bear a child. This situation brings into conflict two fundamental rights—the fetal right to life and the woman's right not to be compelled to become pregnant and to bear a child. The fetus's right to life is certainly not contingent upon how its life was initiated.[68] Yet there is serious question as to how far this right should extend in limiting other rights. While emotional, mental, and physical problems are more likely to arise in rape situations (especially in young girls),[69] such a condition does not lessen the fetal right to life. It is a close question as to which right should prevail in this situation. But the fact that a conflict exists does not mean that one of the conflicting rights must be annihilated. The failure to recognize the fetal right to life is an unfair oversimplification of the problem. The only reasonable solution is to balance the competing rights. Perhaps the woman's right not to be pregnant would be weightier than the fetal right to life in a rape situation. But there is no need to say that because the woman's right outweighs the fetal right in this situation that no fetal right to life can exist. This is lousy reasoning.

The fetal right to life would not be an absolute right that is always superior to all other rights. It would be subject to limitation

---

[68] Should the unborn baby be punished for the actions of his/her parents?

[69] While pregnancies are more dangerous for young girls than for older girls, the emotional damage from abortion is also greater in young girls (*Handbook*, p. 42).

in accordance with due process. The fact that the fetal right to life can be limited is not self-contradictory either. Even born persons can be deprived of life after the demands of due process have been met (e.g., capital punishment). The fundamental problem with *Roe* is that it failed to recognize *any* fetal right to life. A right-to-life amendment would remedy this situation by establishing this right so that it would have to be balanced with conflicting rights before it could be extinguished. The purpose of a right-to-life amendment is just that—to bestow a right to life on fetuses—not to give fetuses every right enjoyed by born persons, and not to give fetuses an absolute right to life. Obviously, the fetal right to life would have to give way to the mother's right to life.

Finally, it should be noted that pregnancies resulting from rape are very rare.[70]

(d) *Pregnancy from intercourse engaged in to avoid divorce.* The Commission showed great imagination in conjuring up this claim. The Commission argued that *if* a woman submitted to intercourse with her husband only once every twelve to eighteen months, and *if* she did so then only to prevent the husband from getting a divorce on the grounds of denial of consortium, then *if* she became pregnant as a result and *if* she wanted an abortion, it would be a denial of her due process rights to deprive her of one. This is a ridiculous chain of *ifs*. Even *if* such a situation were to occur, the woman was never compelled to have intercourse.

2. *Should abortion be a part of family planning?*

(a) *Unprepared parents.* It is argued that abortion saves children from having to live in families that cannot adequately care

---

[70] One ten-year study of 3,500 rape cases in the Minneapolis-St. Paul area revealed no case where pregnancy resulted from rape. "Zero Pregnancies in 3,500 Rapes," *The Educator*, vol. 2, no. 4, Sept. 1970, quoted in *Handbook*, p. 38. Two other studies cited by Dr. Wilke further substantiate the rarity of pregnancy resulting from rape. One study of one thousand rape victims showed no resulting pregnancies. Out of 86,000 consecutive induced abortions in Czechoslovakia, only twenty-two were done for rape victims (*Handbook*, p. 39).

for them or even do not want them. It is felt by some that it would be better to kill the fetus than to allow it to be born with the chance that it would be raised in such an environment. The fetus has a right to be born into a family that will love and care for him or her; this right should be protected. However, it is illogical to say that a fetus has this right unless it also has the right to life itself. The right to have a good and loving home cannot exist unless and until the right to life exists. Both of these rights should be recognized and protected.

(b) *Abortion for the sake of the fetus.* Some say that in some instances it would be best for the fetus to be killed so that it will not be born.[71] This is a version of the euthanasia argument (mercy killing). The problem with this argument is that it is based upon a string of unprovable assumptions, which only an omniscient being could verify. How do we know that a fetus would be better off to be aborted than to be born, just because they would be likely to suffer after being born? Do we know that an unborn child would prefer to be aborted than to be born, just because they would be likely to suffer after being born? Most people suffer before they die, whether this is sooner or later.

(c) *Abstinence.* If a couple does not want and is not prepared to care for a child, then they can either use contraceptives or refrain from sexual intercourse. This is the ideal way to prevent unwanted pregnancies. But once a child is conceived, it is too late to decide the child is not wanted, because at that point, a third independent life is involved. Then the parents have a responsibility to provide for the child.

(d) *Adoption.* In many instances, adoption is an available remedy for unwanted children.[72] However, unwanted pregnancies

---

[71] See paragraph above. See also chapter 8, below, and the discussion of a right of diseased or deformed fetuses not to be conceived.

[72] In *Danforth*, the court held that the father's consent is not required in order for a pregnant woman to have an abortion. However, the father's consent is often required before a child can be put up for adoption. This anomaly makes abortion easier to secure than adoption. To many women, this makes abortion more desirable than adoption, if

do not always result in unwanted babies. A number of studies have been made that conclude that initial feelings about pregnancy are only partially predictive of whether a baby will be wanted and well cared for when born.[73]

(e) *Abused and neglected children*. The problem of child abuse is separate and distinct from the fetal right-to-life question. The fetal right to life is not competing with the child's right to be treated well. Both of these rights should be protected; neither requires that the other be diminished or eliminated. In addition, some studies have shown that the great majority of battered children were "planned pregnancies."[74] This shows that abortion would have only an insignificant impact on reducing the incidents of child abuse.

3. *Defective babies*. Another proabortion argument is that diseased and deformed babies should be prevented from being born, now that science is often able to discover such problems before birth. But, as was pointed out earlier, the right to life is not equated with "meaningful life." That a fetus may experience pain and suffering in the future should not be a basis for denying that fetus the right to live any more than this should deny a living person the right to live. Cures for deformities and diseases should be sought without extinguishing the right to live. Nevertheless, it is acknowledged that in some instances of severe deformity, where a child will not have the ability to survive after birth, that abortion may be justified.

---

they have decided not to keep the baby. This double standard promotes abortion. On the other hand, the black market is beginning to operate once again. Because of the great demand for babies to adopt, some women are selling their babies themselves rather than going through governmental adoption agencies. This allows the mother to receive the adoption money rather than the state. "More and More Couples Wishing to Adopt Eye Black Market," Provo *Daily Herald*, December 19, 1976, p. 86; and "N.Y. Probes Baby Sales for Profit," UPI Press Release, Provo *Daily Herald*, December 26, 1976.

[73] *Handbook*, pp. 57–58.

[74] *Handbook*, pp. 59–60.

D. A Woman's Equal Protection Rights—The Poor

The Commission stated in finding number six:

> The proposed constitutional amendments are inconsistent with the Fourteenth Amendment. To prohibit abortion would be a denial of equal protection to poor women, among whom racial and ethnic minority women are disproportionately represented. (Report, p. 99)

The equal protection clause does not require that poor and rich people be given equal opportunity to break the law. If a right-to-life amendment is passed, it would become almost impossible for poor women to get abortions, while wealthier women would be able to travel somewhere to get a legal abortion, or else they could pay a high fee to get an illegal abortion. Admittedly, this would be an unequal standard, but it would not deny poor women of equal protection of the law. The law applies equally to both classes of women.[75] No one has a right to be afforded an equal opportunity to get an abortion if it is illegal. For the Commission to have turned this into a racial issue is pathetic and disgraceful.

---

[75] One of the world's foremost leaders in providing birth control and abortion information for the poor was Margaret Sanger (1879–1966). She is regarded as the founder of Planned Parenthood. She played a major role in the long road to recognizing women's rights, including reproductive rights, in America. Students of law and history will appreciate the historical summary of her life made by Planned Parenthood, titled "Margaret Sanger—Our Founder," accessed on May 10, 2020 at: https://www.plannedparenthood.org/files/9214/7612/8734/Sanger_Fact_Sheet_Oct_2016.pdf. This article provides a concise summary of many of the profound issues that have brought First Amendment freedom of speech protection for legitimate information about sexual reproduction during the last one hundred years. Langer's work was also instrumental in the legalizing of contraceptives (through the *Griswold v. Connecticut* case). Ms. Sanger is criticized by Planned Parenthood for the role she took in support of eugenics and ableism. Sanger was named by *Life* magazine as one of the one hundred most important people in the twentieth century.

E. The Right to Limit Childbearing

The Civil Rights Commission recommended to Congress the following:

> Congress should reject constitutional amendments which seek to abolish the historic freedom to limit childbearing as contained in the Bill of Rights and the Fourteenth Amendment and as recognized by the Supreme Court of the United States.
>
> Congress should reject anti-abortion legislation and amendments, and repeal those which have been enacted, which undermine the constitutional right to limit childbearing. (Report, p. 101)

Families have always enjoyed the right to limit childbearing through abstinence, but the right to limit childbearing at the expense of the fetus's right to life has only existed since the Supreme Court announced its *Roe v. Wade* decision in 1973. A right-to-life amendment would only prevent a couple from limiting childbearing in ways that would infringe upon the fetal right to life. And if a women's life would be seriously jeopardized through childbirth, her right to have an abortion would prevail over the fetus's right to life. A right-to-life amendment would not prohibit the use of contraceptives to prevent conception; it would only prohibit the unwarranted killing of conceived human life.

F. The Right to Unlimited Childbearing

It is said that because *Roe* gives a woman the right to decide whether or not to terminate a pregnancy, that *Roe* can be relied on in the future to prevent the government from limiting the size of our families. This interpretation of *Roe* is possible, but not likely. *Roe* held that a woman's right to make a decision about abortion can be restricted by the state because of the state's interest in the mother's health and in potential human life. It is possible that the state's right could be extended, relying on *Roe*, so that a state could terminate fetal life if it feels that any increase in population would be detrimental to the state. This is especially foreseeable because abortion has become a safe procedure and because there is presently no fetal right to life. But it does not follow that *Roe* would in any way support a government mandate that *Roe* gives women the right to have many children.

Because *Roe* legalized abortion, in the future abortion could be a legal way for the state to limit childbearing. The state can already compel individuals to be vaccinated.[76] If enough people begin to feel the United States is overcrowded, the *Roe* precedent could require abortion to be used as a type of vaccine to prevent overpopulation. Passage of a fetal right-to-life amendment could prohibit the state from limiting the population by compelling abortions, but *Roe* does not provide this.

A year prior to the *Roe* decision, in *Eisenstadt v. Baird*, 405 U.S. 438 (1972), the Supreme Court said:

> If the right of privacy means anything, it is the right of the individual married or single, to be free from unwarranted governmental intrusion into matters so fundamentally affecting a person as the decision whether to bear or beget a child. (405 U.S. at 453)

Eisenstadt and *Roe* establish the right to *limit* childbearing through contraception and abortion. These cases could be interpreted to give an individual the right to have as many children as she chooses. Nevertheless, having this right does not necessarily entail having the right to have *unlimited* children.

Having children is a *public* as well as a *private* matter, in that

---

[76] *Jacobson v. Massachusetts*, 197 U.S. 11 (1905).

one person's children have an impact on society as well as the parents. The results of using contraceptives and abortifacients are more private than the failure to use them because their use will not result in more children, which could burden society. Thus, while *Eisenstadt* and *Roe* have established that the use of contraceptives and abortifacients is a private matter, the failure to use them may be held to be a public matter—thus justifying the state to compel their usage to limit families. These cases, therefore, could be used either to strengthen or weaken a woman's right to have as many children as she wants. But in no way is *Roe* needed to preserve a right to unlimited childbearing.

G. Overpopulation

Fear of overpopulation is one of the arguments used in support of abortion.[77] Experts are divided on whether in fact the world is overpopulated. Some nations have passed birth control laws to limit the number of children a couple can have. It is possible that in future years the question of whether a state may limit the size of families

---

[77] One example of the overpopulation argument is given by Paul Pruyser. The facts, however, do not bear out that an overpopulation problem actually exists. Pruyser wrote:

> The Biblical exhortation to "be fruitful and multiply" may have been constructive in an agrarian society with a high mortality rate, but it is becoming destructive in today's world. To take this text out of context and to turn it into an everlasting moral injunction is a pernicious form of fundamentalism, pernicious because it fails to come to grips with the moral issue involved in self-duplication. That issue is no longer whether I can survive in my offspring, whether my family or tribe or nation can survive, but whether mankind can survive. The solution of this will require, among other things, an entirely new theology of propagation, based upon a fresh assessment of the relations between the individual and other species, and the role of man in the whole order of creation. (Paul Pruyser, "A Psychological View of Religion in the 1970's," quoted in Elliott Silverstein, "From Comstockery through Population Control: The Inevitability of Balancing," *N. C. Central L. J.* 6:8, 40 [Fall 1974]).

may come before the Supreme Court. However, even if the issue were eventually decided against the right of a family to have as many children as it wants, this should not mean that fetal rights can be extinguished.

Blaming many of the world's problems on overpopulation is a simplistic and often erroneous conclusion. Research done by many experts points to many factors as contributing to world poverty—for example, pollution, lack of education, inferior agricultural practices, and so on. Many experts feel that controlling population growth would have only a marginal effect in reducing these problems.[78] Roger Revelle, a Harvard population expert, reported that deaths resulting from malnutrition had been declining for several decades in the face of a rising population.[79] Many experts agreed that more arable land can be cropped than is now being done.[80] Unquestionably, the nations of the world need to continue making technological advances in agriculture and nutrition education.

Actually, the rate of population growth in America presents a different problem. If our birth rate continues at a rate below replacement level, which it has done since 1973, we may face an

---

[78] *Handbook*, 63–78. Dr. Wilke has compiled data from a number of different sources that support this, some of whom will be specifically referred to later in the text.

[79] *Family Planning Perspectives*, April, 1971, p. 67, referred to in *Handbook*, 74.

[80] Henry Kissinger, AP Report, 1974 World Food Conference, Rome, quoted in *Handbook*, 75. Mr. Kissinger is reported to have said: "Ironically, but fortunately, it is the nations with the most rapidly growing recent food deficits which also possess the greatest capacity for increased production .... For example, worldwide, 42% of potentially arable land is cropped, but in Latin America only 17% is used .... [T]he crop yield can be increased."

One expert has calculated that the world's farmers can support a population forty times greater than today's world population (Prof. Donald Bogue, *Time* magazine, September 13, 1971, quoted in *Handbook*, 74).

See also, Ned H. Greenwood, *Human Environment and Natural Systems* (Belmont, California: Wadsworth Publishing Co. 1973) 107: "Very little is known about the capacity of the earth as a whole to produce food. There are three general approaches to increasing this capacity: new lands can be cultivated; agriculture on lands already under cultivation can be intensified by conventional means; and new sources and techniques of food production can be developed."

underpopulation that would have a serious economic impact on the nation.[81] As was stated in a 1976 editorial, at present rates, our population will double in fifty-seven years.[82] This editorial brought out that our 1977 birth rate was greater than the death rate (3:2 ratio)[83] and that many foreigners were coming here and remaining illegally. This view, however, does not account for the following: (1) in a very few years, the death rate will increase when the population bulge reaches old age; (2) the national birth rate continues to decline;[84] and (3) immigration laws can be more strictly enforced, and quotas can be reduced.

H. Undesirable Social Effects of Abortion[85]

The Commission concluded:

> No one has suggested that abortion is a violation of social duties or subversive of good order. If Congress could establish that having an abortion at any stage

---

[81] President Nixon's National Goals Research Staff, "Toward Balanced Growth: Quantity with Quality" (Washington, DC: Government Printing Office 1970), reported in *Handbook*, 66–68.

[82] Editorial, "A View on Population Growth," Provo *Daily Herald*, December 31, 1976, p. 17.

[83] In 2019, the US birth rate dropped to approximately 12 per one thousand per year, and the death rate was approximately 9 per one thousand; this is a 4:3 ratio.
   In 1977, the US birth rate was approximately 15 per one thousand people per year, and the death rate was approximately 10 per one thousand people per year. The US birth rate declined to a record low 14.8 births per one thousand persons, continuing a trend since 1972 when the birth rate was 15.6 per one thousand persons. Before 1972, the lowest birthrate was 16.6 in 1936 .... Provisional data through October (1976) show a further decline in fertility (National Center for Health Statistics, UPI Press Release, Provo *Daily Herald*, December 31, 1976, p. 13).

[84] *Id.*

[85] Some of the desirable effects of legalized abortion are a reduced illegitimate birth rate, fewer pregnancy-caused marriages, and fewer illegal abortions (Foote, *supra*, at 525).

of pregnancy was, even though a protected exercise of religion, a violation of social duties or subversive of good order, Congress could outlaw abortions from the moment of conception without regard to the First Amendment. (Report, p. 37)

There are a number of social problems subversive of good order that may reasonably be said to stem from legalized abortion that would justify prohibiting abortion, completely apart from the fetal right to life. Abortion (1) promotes a disregard for human life and other life; (2) promotes extramarital sex and other immoral and illegal conduct; (3) is destructive of healthy family life by promoting extramarital sex; and (4) promotes selfishness. Although these reasons would be secondary to the fetal right to life, they are independently sufficient to justify such a law. Justice Harlan said in his concurring opinion in *Alberts v. California,* 354 U.S. 476 (1957) (companion case to *Roth v. United States*):

> It seems clear that it is not irrational, in our present state of knowledge, to consider that pornography can induce a type of sexual conduct which a State may deem obnoxious to the moral fabric of society .... The State can reasonably draw the inference that over a long period of time indiscriminate dissemination of materials, the essential character of which is to degrade sex, will have an eroding effect on moral standards. And the State has a legitimate interest in protecting the privacy of the home against the invasion of unsolicited obscenity. (354 U.S. at 501–502)

The rationale that allows a state to completely suppress obscene materials is perfectly applicable justification for prohibiting abortion as well—"to protect 'the social interest in order and morality.'"[86] The court held in *Paris Adult Theatre I v. Slaton*, 413 U.S. 49 (1973) that "[t]he States have the power to make a morally neutral judgment that public exhibition of obscene material, … has a tendency to injure the community as a whole, to endanger the public safety, or to jeopardize (in Chief Justice Warren's words) the States' 'right [to] maintain a decent society.'" A state's right to maintain a decent society would certainly encompass a right to proscribe abortion as well as obscenity.[87]

---

[86] *Paris Adult Theatre I v. Slaton*, 413 U.S. 49, 61 (1973), citing *Roth, supra*.

[87] Once a right to life amendment is passed, it would not be necessary to prove a connection between abortion and antisocial behavior or societal ills. But until then, it is. Obstetrician Paul E. Lewis, MD, said: "Multiple abortions increase the risk of very preterm delivery, especially if the abortions are done later in the pregnancy. This is supported by data from Korea, where abortion is often used as birth control" (Interview with Dr. Lewis, May 9, 2020.)

The court in *Roe* described the right to have an abortion as a "fundamental" right (410 U.S. 155). Until passage of a right to life amendment, a state cannot prohibit an abortion without satisfying the Supreme Court's "compelling interest" test.

After passage of a right to life amendment, a state could prohibit abortions based upon a reasonable belief that abortion causes societal problems. Then the burden would be on the one seeking an abortion to prove that there is no reasonable connection between abortion and its bad effects (413 U.S. at 60–61).

CHAPTER FIVE

Aftermath of Roe v. Wade

A. Tax-Funded Abortions

On June 20, 1977, the Supreme Court decided the case of *Beal v. Doe*, 432 U.S. 438, and held that a state is not required to finance nontherapeutic abortions (i.e., abortions other than to save the life of the mother). In *Maher v. Roe*, 432 U.S. 464, decided the same day, the Court held that the federal government is likewise not required to finance nontherapeutic abortions.

In 1976, the federal government was spending $40 – 45 million for between 250,000 and 300,000 abortions. In September 1976, a majority of both houses of Congress voted not to use taxpayers' money to finance abortions, except where the mother's health would be endangered by not having an abortion.[88] A majority of Congress believed that taxpayers should not have to pay for unnecessary (nontherapeutic) abortions, which a majority of taxpayers believe is

---

[88] It is not certain whether this congressional, HEW appropriations law would have financed abortions done for the treatment of rape and incest victims. Representative Silvia O. Conte (R. Mass.) said: "It will be up to HEW to interpret this" (*Congressional Quarterly*, September 18, 1976, p. 2541).

immoral. Opponents argued that Congress's failure to provide such funds would deprive poor women of their right to have an abortion.

In upholding Congress's policy, the Court held that the governmental policy favoring birth over abortion justified its refusal to finance nontherapeutic abortions. Some of the dissenting justices felt that this decision is inconsistent with *Roe v. Wade*. A majority of Justices, however, disagreed.

Regardless of whether these cases were or were not consistent with *Roe*, these developments represented a significant victory for fetal rights. First, they indicated that a majority of Americans personally opposed abortion. Support for a right-to-life amendment was growing then. Second, these cases indicated that the Court was willing to place some limits on the right to have an abortion. Of course, these cases still did not recognize a fetal right to life, nor in reality did they provide much protection at all to fetuses.

B. Spousal or Parental Consent Not Required for an Abortion

In *Planned Parenthood of Central Missouri v. Danforth*, 428 U.S. 52 (1976), the Supreme Court held that provisions of a state statute requiring spousal consent and parental consent for minors were unconstitutional. This holding was not surprising. Were the woman's right to have an abortion contingent upon spousal or parental consent, it really would not be the woman's right—it would be a family right. If the right of the unborn child cannot restrict the mother's right to an abortion, it would indeed be anomalous to allow the spouse or parents to restrict this right.[89]

The Court in *Danforth* upheld that part of the Missouri statute

---

[89] There now exists, however, a double standard, in that many current adoption procedures require the father's consent, while this consent is not required to have an abortion. This situation makes abortion easier to procure than adoptions, and to that extent, it encourages abortion more than adoption.

that protected fetal life from the point of viability, 428 U.S. 63. Finally, the Court held unconstitutional the provision prohibiting the saline amniocentesis abortion procedure after the first twelve weeks of pregnancy. This Missouri statute attempted to comply with both the *Roe v. Wade* edict and at the same time to protect fetuses as much as possible. But the Court found that the provision prohibiting saline amniocentesis was an arbitrary regulation that would prohibit the most commonly used abortion procedure, the one that was supposedly even safer than childbirth. This holding is not surprising either. If a woman has a right to an abortion, it seems only logical that she be able to choose any safe abortion procedure that she wishes.

These extensions of the right to an abortion logically follow from the *Roe v. Wade* decision. However, the Court made one extension of *Roe* in the *Danforth* case that was absolutely disgusting. Section 6(1) of the Missouri statute in question required physicians to exercise professional care to preserve the lives of all born and aborted fetuses. Missouri did not intend to prevent abortion by this provision but merely to protect fetal life as much as possible after abortion. Missouri's attempt to prohibit saline amniocentesis abortions was related to Section 6(1) in that it attempted to prohibit abortions once a fetus had developed to a point where it had a better chance to be born alive. However, unlike the prohibition of saline amniocentesis abortions, the Section 6(1) requirements did not interfere at all with the woman's right to have an abortion. But the Court chose not to interpret it this way; it held that Section 6(1) violated the woman's right to have an abortion.[90] The Court's interpretation was clearly erroneous; the provision was only meant to protect those fetuses that were still alive after the abortion. Missouri's intended construction did not conflict with the right to an abortion. But, had the Court upheld Section 6(1), it would have established a right to life for fetuses

---

[90] The Court held that the protection given fetuses in Section 6(1) would prohibit physicians from performing most abortions. The Court said that, as applied to previable fetuses, this *protection* violated the woman's right to have an abortion.

who survive abortion. The Court defended its ruling by arguing that if the Missouri law were allowed to stand, that this would interfere with the woman's right to have an abortion. No! That's not right. Once the fetus is delivered from the womb alive, it is a live human being—it is no longer a fetus. But the Supreme Court disagreed; it ruled that the fetus continues to be a fetus after a failed abortion and that it does not become a "person" if the fetus survives an attempt to kill it through an abortion. This is a reprehensible and repulsive ruling. This is a dilemma that often attends partial-birth abortion, and it is one of the reasons why eventually a law was passed outlawing it. In 2003, Congress passed and President Bush signed into law the Partial Birth Abortion Ban Act (18 U.S.C. § 1531). (See also discussion below on page 74.)

In *Friendship Medical Center, Ltd. v. Chicago Board of Health*, 505 F.2d 1141 (1975), the Seventh Circuit Court of Appeals invalidated a law requiring abortion clinics to satisfy certain minimal health regulations, such as being equipped with oxygen. As a result, safety and health requirements for abortion clinics need only satisfy nominal requirements.[91]

In *Bigelow v. Virginia*, 421 U.S. 809 (1975), the Supreme Court invalidated a state law prohibiting the advertising of abortion services. Prior to *Roe*, this type of commercial speech could be prohibited in order to protect society from the detrimental effects of abortion. But now that the Court has established the right to have an abortion, abortion propaganda can be widely disseminated to convince women to have abortions.

In 1992, a Pennsylvania law that put various restrictions on abortion was challenged, and the Supreme Court struck down parts of that law in *Planned Parenthood v. Casey*, 505 U.S. 833 (1992). *Casey* affirmed the 1976 *Danforth* case, which had previously struck down spousal and parental consent requirements. *Casey* also struck down

---

[91] The Court held that because the health requirements to be met by abortion clinics were more stringent than those to be met by other "dispensaries," the requirements violated the equal protection clause of the Fourteenth Amendment.

a waiting period requirement, and *Casey* reinforced the 1989 *Webster* case, in which the Supreme Court rejected the trimester framework in favor of the viability standard for when a state can begin to protect fetal life. However, probably the most significant thing about the *Casey* case was what it revealed about the positions of each of the nine justices about *Roe*. Justices Rehnquist, White, Scalia, and Thomas wanted *Roe* to be overturned. But while seven of the justices were appointed by Republican presidents, three of those justices declined to support repeal of *Roe*—Justices Kennedy, Souter, and O'Connor. This was one of the first cases where the conservatives came to realize that Justice Souter was not the conservative they thought he was. And Justices O'Connor and Kennedy both backed away from previous positions, where they had expressed a willingness to limit or even overturn *Roe*.

C. Mother Charged with Drug Abuse for Baby Born Addicted to Cocaine

The Associated Press reported in December 1988 that a Florida woman was being charged with child abuse and a felony drug charge in connection with giving birth to a baby boy born addicted to cocaine. The news service reported that the mother admitted taking cocaine almost daily throughout her pregnancy. In prior, similar cases, mothers of addicted babies have been charged with child abuse in connection with prenatal drug ingestion. But this appears to be the first case where such a mother is also charged with distributing a controlled substance to someone else where the recipient is a baby born with a drug addiction. The state prosecutors planned to argue that the illegal distribution took place after the mother ingested it, when her body internally transmitted it to the baby.

I did not follow the outcome of this case, but the mother in this case certainly argued that the *Roe v. Wade* decision barred her from liability of this nature, since it gives her a right to decide whether or not to abort the fetus. The respective rights of mother and infant in such a case are currently a matter of debate. For example, in November 1988, the Illinois Supreme Court dismissed a lawsuit where a father, on behalf of his child, sued the mother for prenatal injuries negligently inflicted on the child by the mother. The court refused to recognize such a cause of action against the mother:

> Holding a mother liable for the unintentional infliction of prenatal injuries subjects to state scrutiny all the decisions a woman must make in attempting to carry a pregnancy to term and infringes on her right to privacy and bodily autonomy .... The relationship between a pregnant woman and her fetus is unlike the relationship between any other plaintiff and defendant. No other plaintiff depends exclusively on any other defendant for everything necessary for life itself. No other defendant must go through the biological changes of the most profound type, possibly at the risk of her own life, in order to bring forth an adversary into the world.[92]

However, the Illinois case could be distinguished from the Florida cocaine addiction case, if Florida could show that the mother knew that her conduct was likely to cause serious harm to her baby.

Currently, there exists a significant contradiction in the laws of those states that guarantee that a child be born with a certain quality of life, because this is at odds with the *Roe v. Wade* ruling that denies that a fetus has the right to be born at all. This anomaly in the area of fetal rights did not exist prior to the 1973 *Roe v. Wade* decision. The Supreme Court's ruling in that case extinguished the fetal right to life. The successful prosecution of this case and a conviction of the baby's mother would have stood in bold defiance of *Roe v. Wade*.

---

[92] *Stallman v. Youngquist*, 125 Ill.2d 267, 278, 531 N.E.2d 355 (1988).

D. Viability Standard Established—
The Webster Case

In 1989, sixteen years after the Supreme Court decided *Roe v. Wade*, the Court released its ruling in *Webster v. Reproductive Health Services*, 492 U.S. 490 (1989). *Webster* reaffirmed and reinforced the Court's ruling in *Danforth* (1976) that allowed states to protect fetal life beginning at the point of viability. In 1989, it appeared that the *Webster* case signaled a willingness on the part of the Supreme Court to reverse *Roe* and recognize a fetal right to life. It didn't turn out that way, but the case did resolve one of the conflicts or ambiguities that *Roe* created.

Chief Justice Rehnquist's plurality opinion (joined by Justices White and Kennedy)[93] contained the words that seemed to reflect the court's willingness to protect fetal life (492 U.S. at 519):

> [W]e do not see why the State's interest in protecting potential human life should come into existence only at the point of viability [when a fetus is able to survive outside of the mother's womb], and that there should therefore be a rigid line allowing state regulation after viability but prohibiting it before viability.

This statement was an indication by four of the justices that they were ready to move in the direction of reversing or modifying *Roe*. A fifth Justice, Sandra O'Connor, hinted that she would go along with those four if the right case came along.[94] While she did state

---

[93] Justice Scalia concurred with Justice Rehnquist's conclusions but for different reasons; he would have overturned *Roe*.

[94] Chief Justice Rehnquist pointed out in his opinion in *Webster* that Justice O'Connor had previously stated her opinion that state interests in protecting potential human life exist throughout the pregnancy (492 U.S. at 519). But Justice O'Connor didn't repeat this statement in *Webster*; instead, she said that the case should be resolved on a different basis. As it turns out, Justice O'Connor was backing away from giving extended protection to

her dissatisfaction with the trimester scheme established by the *Roe v. Wade* ruling (492 U.S. at 529), that was as far as she would go. She approached the *Webster* case with deliberate judicial restraint, putting off a confrontation with the big issue until another day.

Webster resolved a conflict created by *Roe v. Wade* as to when a state could begin to protect fetal life—(a) beginning in the third trimester of a pregnancy or (b) beginning when a fetus becomes viable.

1. *Summary of specific findings and rulings in the* Webster *case.* There are two main parts of the Supreme Court's ruling in *Webster.* First, it upheld the right of states to make it unlawful for public facilities, employees, or funds to be used to perform abortions, except when necessary to save the life of the mother. Second, it held that states can make laws to protect human life from the moment of viability and can require a medical determination to be made of the viability of any fetus after twenty weeks in gestation (a time often prior to viability) (492 U.S. 515–520).The significance of this latter aspect of the ruling is: (i) it discards *Roe's* third trimester rule as to criteria for determining when a state can begin to protect fetal life; (ii) it reaffirms that the point of viability is the time when a state can protect fetal life; and (iii) it now establishes that at an earlier point in pregnancy, when the fetus has potential viability, a state can begin to require tests to be made to determine the viability of a fetus, if a woman wants an abortion.

None of these specific holdings represents a significant departure from previous Supreme Court rulings. But the reasoning of five of the current nine justices indicated that the court might revise *Roe v. Wade* in the future.

---

fetuses. By the time *Planned Parenthood v. Casey* came to the court in 1992, Justice O'Connor had become more protective of a woman's right to an abortion.

2. *An examination of the justices' opinions and what this could have meant for abortion and fetal rights laws in the future.* An examination of the justices' different opinions shed light on what the justices were willing to consider in the future.

Justices Rehnquist, White, and Kennedy would allow states to protect fetal life before viability, perhaps from the moment of conception. They would narrow but not overturn *Roe*.

Justice Scalia would agree with Justices Rehnquist, White, and Kennedy in allowing states to protect fetal rights, but he would overturn *Roe*. This would run the risk of erasing privacy rights of women that *Roe* recognized.

Justice O'Connor's opinion is somewhat of a mystery because she implied that she would consider overturning *Roe* if the right case presented, but she declined to do so in this case, which did present such an opportunity. She hinted that she might extend the right of states to protect fetal life prior to viability, although perhaps not all the way back to conception because this would violate a couple's right to use contraceptives that take effect after conception. She said that such an extension would require overturning *Griswold v. Connecticut,* which she would be reluctant to do.

Justices Blackmun, Brennan, and Marshall expressed protest and alarm at the opinions of Rehnquist and Scalia. They warned that *Roe* was in serious jeopardy; they denounced what they saw as the Court's willingness to overturn *Roe* in the near future.

Justice Stevens aligned himself with Justices Blackmun, Brennan, and Marshall, but he also expressed agreement with Justice O'Connor that if the Court expanded the right of states to protect fetal life before viability, that this would jeopardize a couple's right to use contraceptives that was recognized in *Griswold*.

3. *Aftermath of* Webster. Ultimately, the Supreme Court never got any closer to making a significant modification of *Roe v. Wade*. The right case never came along, and the composition of the Court

became more protective of the right to an abortion beginning in the early 1990s, during the administration of President Bill Clinton.

Following the death of liberal Justice Thurgood Marshall in 1990, President George H. W. Bush nominated Clarence Thomas to replace him. Although Thomas was black (as was Justice Marshall), Thomas was a conservative, while Marshall was a staunch liberal. The Senate confirmation process of Thomas became a nasty and prolonged battle, where the Senate Democrats accused Thomas of many things, including sexual harassment. One of the points of contention in the confirmation process was Thomas's position on *Roe v. Wade*. Thomas declined to get drawn into a specific discussion about *Roe*, but there was a strong outcry of the Democrats that the president better not nominate someone who would dare to overturn *Roe*. This threat and alarm that took place during the confirmation process for Justice Thomas has taken place during the confirmation proceedings for every Supreme Court nominee ever since. There has been and continues to be a very loud and vocal group of people who rail against anyone who would dare to modify or repeal *Roe*. This has become a powerful force, protecting *Roe* from every possible attack. This force has been effective in helping to build widespread support for *Roe*, which has continued to be effective until today.

Another thing that happened after *Webster* was the addition of two powerful liberal justices to the Court during the Clinton administration—Justice Ruth Bader Ginsburg (in 1993, replacing conservative Byron White) and Justice Stephen Breyer (in 1997, replacing Blackmun [author of the *Roe v. Wade* opinion]). The result of this was that during the Clinton administration, the slim prospect for recognizing a fetal right to life evaporated; the composition of the Court became more proabortion than pro-life.

Thereafter, during the administration of George W. Bush (2001–2008), the Court held a slight conservative majority of 5–4 in most cases, except that Justice Kennedy would sometimes vote with the liberal wing.

While the Court hinted a willingness to reverse or modify *Roe* in 1989, no significant modification ever materialized. Subsequent to *Webster*, the court has not made any significant limitations of the holding in *Roe v. Wade*.

E. Partial-Birth Abortion Ban

In the 1990s, Congress passed bans on partial-birth abortions twice during the Clinton administration, but President Clinton vetoed both of them. On November 5, 2003, President George W. Bush signed into law the Partial Birth Abortion Ban Act, 18 U.S.C. §1531. The law was challenged, but it was upheld by the Supreme Court in *Gonzalez v. Carhart*, 550 U.S. 124 (2007).

This federal law prohibits partial-birth abortions except if necessary to protect the mother's life. The law does not have an exception to protect the mother's health. The law has been interpreted to prohibit the dilation and extraction (D&X) abortion method. Some states have enacted similar laws.

F. Unborn Child Pain Awareness Bills

During the last sixteen years, there have been a number of bills introduced in Congress that would provide for pain-reducing drugs to be provided to the child/fetus being aborted. Bills were introduced in 2004, 2005, 2006, 2007, 2010, and 2013. These bills were titled Unborn Child Pain Awareness Act, and the House passed the 2013 bill, but it died in the Senate. Twenty-five state legislatures have considered similar legislation.[95]

---

[95] https://en.wikipedia.org/wiki/Prental_perception. Accessed April 6, 2020.

CHAPTER SIX

Gay Rights and Same-Sex Marriage

A. Anti-sodomy Laws Invalidated

Initially, the application of *Roe* was limited primarily to areas of women's rights and the regulation of abortions. In 1976, a gay couple argued unsuccessfully that *Roe* required the court to invalidate a Virginia anti-sodomy law. In *Doe v. Commonwealth's Attorney for City of Richmond*, 425 U.S. 901 (1976), the Supreme Court upheld an anti-sodomy law that prohibited homosexuals from having sexual relations.[96] The plaintiffs had argued that the law was unconstitutional as applied to male homosexual relations with another male, consensually and in private. It was argued that *Roe* stood for the principle that every individual has a right to be free from unwarranted governmental intrusion into one's decisions on private matters of intimate concern, such as "[p]rivate consensual sex acts between adults" that are not harmful and in which the state has no legitimate interest. The Supreme Court disagreed with this view and affirmed the district court's decision. That decision had construed the constitutional right of sexual privacy to be limited

---

[96] The Supreme Court affirmed the US District Court for the Eastern District of Virginia with only a one-sentence statement.

to "the privacy of the incidents of marriage," "the sanctity of the home," and "the nurture of family life." Because homosexuality "is obviously no portion of marriage, home or family life," it may be prohibited even when in the privacy of the home in order to promote "morality and decency" (*Doe v. Commonwealth's Attorney*, 403 F. Supp. 1199 [E. D. Va. 1975]).

This case was important because it upheld a law that prohibited homosexual relations and because it reaffirmed that marriage was only between a man and a woman. Traditionally, the primary purpose of marriage has been to provide the best possible environment for the rearing of children. A corollary to this has been the principle that intimate sexual relations should be exclusively reserved for within marriage. Today, however, because contraceptives and abortifacients can now eliminate all unwanted, illegitimate children, the argument that extramarital sex is detrimental to children has been greatly weakened. Now, many people even preach the need for premarital sex. The *Doe v. Commonwealth* decision, however, strengthened both of those traditional values: that marriage is an important social institution and that sexual relations should be reserved for traditional marriages.[97]

But twenty-seven years later, in *Lawrence v. Texas*, 539 U.S. 558 (2003), the Supreme Court used the *Roe* case as a basis for invalidating a similar Texas anti-sodomy law. Then, in 2015, the Supreme Court also used *Roe* as a basis for invalidating laws in all states that prohibited same-sex marriages (*Obergefell v. Hodges*, 576 U.S. ____).

When the Constitution was ratified in 1788, the regulation of

---

[97] Although *Doe v. Commonwealth* was subsequently affirmed and bolstered by the Supreme Court in *Bowers v. Hardwick*, 478 U.S. 186 (1986), less than twenty years later, the Supreme Court reversed itself and specifically overturned *Bowers v. Hardwick* (and *Doe v. Commonwealth*) by its decision in *Lawrence v. Texas*, 539 U.S. 558 (2003). In *Lawrence*, for the first time, the Court recognized a personal "liberty" under the due process clause of the Fourteenth Amendment to engage in consensual, same-sex relations. The Court said that this liberty was part of the right to privacy that was identified in *Griswold, Eisenstadt,* and *Roe*. Finally, in 2015, the Supreme Court struck down laws that made same-sex marriage illegal (*Obergefell v. Hodges*, 576 U.S. ____).

marriage was a state matter. It was undisputed then that the federal government had no power to regulate marriage, divorce, adultery, fornication, or any other matters pertaining to relations between the sexes. But this changed dramatically in the 1960s. Supreme Court rulings from 1965 to 2015 have drastically altered most aspects of relationships between the sexes, and the *Roe v. Wade* decision of 1973 is the foundation of this major shift in governmental power from the states to the federal government.

This shift in power led to two initiatives intended to correct it, the Defense of Marriage Act of 1996 and the Federal Marriage Amendment that was introduced in Congress in 2003. Neither of these initiatives is a part of our current laws, but an understanding of those political efforts helps to understand the impact that *Roe* has had on American law.

B. The Defense of Marriage Act Invalidated

The Defense of Marriage Act (DOMA) was passed into law by Congress in 1996, at a time when a few states began to consider passing laws to recognize same-sex marriages. The DOMA says that states do not have to recognize same-sex marriages made in another state. This set up a future battle between DOMA and the full faith and credit clause of the Constitution, the latter which requires states to recognize the validity of acts of sister states unless such laws are repulsive to a particular state.

The DOMA was struck down by the Supreme Court by a 5–4 vote in 2013 in the case of *United States v. Windsor*, 570 U.S. 744. The position of all the justices in this case followed the predictable liberal/conservative split, with Justice Kennedy providing the swing vote and writing the majority opinion. This case is another case of judicial activism and pathetic reasoning. The rationale endorsed by a majority of justices in this case has damaged and weakened the rule of law and the Constitution. The Court demolished its long-standing principles of standing, and it invalidated the DOMA by imputing to Congress speculative and false intentions that were irrelevant in the first place. The *Windsor* case stands as one of the most opprobrious Supreme Court decisions of all time.

Before getting to the heart of the substantive issues with the DOMA, the court had to deal with the question of whether the appealing party had standing to appeal the case. It appears that the majority was so anxious to strike down DOMA that it hastily and erroneously ruled that the appealing parties *did* have standing. But the Court got it wrong on the standing issue as well as on the DOMA issue. Here's what happened.

1. *Facts and standing.* Edith Windsor and her gay partner married in Canada. They were living in New York when the partner died in 2009. Windsor received all of her partner spouse's estate. But she had to pay a federal estate tax of $363,053. The Defense of Marriage Act prevented Windsor from having the benefit of the marital deduction. Windsor sued in federal court to have DOMA held unconstitutional and for the IRS to refund the tax she paid. Windsor won her case, which was affirmed by the Second Circuit Court of Appeals. But the IRS still didn't refund her money. Then the IRS and Windsor both appealed to the Supreme Court—they both agreed with the lower court's ruling. There was no legal issue to appeal. All that remained was for the lower Court to order the IRS to pay up; there was no remaining case or controversy for the court to address. It is apparent (as Justice Scalia pointed out in his dissent) that the liberal justices on the Court were so anxious to rule on the merits of the DOMA that they dispensed with the standing requirements.

2. *Supreme Court announces a new legal basis for creating new rights.* Once the Court got to the merits of the DOMA, they proceeded to make an additional, equally flawed ruling in order to strike down the DOMA. Here's a brief summary of their substantive analysis. A majority of the Supreme Court concluded that when Congress and the president enacted the DOMA in 1996, they did so having hatred and

malice toward gays and with the intent to punish gays. Therefore, the Court went on to conclude the DOMA is unconstitutional because such malicious legislative action violates a liberty protected by the Fifth Amendment's due process clause. For the gays who disapprove of DOMA, they herald this ruling; but for those who understand the constitutional principles that the Court has followed for more than two hundred years, the majority's rationale is a total departure from the Court's acknowledged precedents and principles. I will explain.

First, the Court based its holding on a finding that those who enacted DOMA did so with malice and hatred toward gays (Scalia, at 795–798). There is no factual basis for this. And even if there were, such intent would not invalidate the law (Scalia, at 795, citing *United States v. O'Brien*, 391 U.S. 367, 383 [1968]). The majority based its ruling on factual errors and did so without articulating a legal analysis to support its conclusion. The latter point is worth highlighting; the Court's holding was not the result of sound reasoning—it was merely an erroneous edict.

Second, the Court stated that its ruling was based upon a liberty that is protected by the due process clause of the Fifth Amendment. The only other case I know of that was based upon this argument was *Lawrence v. Texas,* 539 U.S. 558 (2003), which ruled that a state cannot criminalize private, consensual sex acts between people of the same sex. The Court cited *Roe* as precedent for this. (See, e.g., 539 U.S. at 565–566.) The Fifth Amendment liberty argument was new in that case, and now it has been invoked again ten years later in another case about gay rights. In these two cases, the Supreme Court has come up with a new expansive theory to create whatever new right it wishes to recognize. Prior to these two cases, under the Court's interpretation of the due process clause, previously unidentified substantive rights had to meet certain requirements before the Court would recognize such rights. For example, previously they would have had to prove that the newly recognized right is "deeply rooted in this Nation's history and tradition" (539 U.S. at 588, J.

Scalia, dissenting). In this ruling (*Windsor*), the court dispensed with the long-established principles that guard against recognizing as a constitutional right any whim of a majority of the Justices.

The Court never even got to the full faith and credit clause argument that I had been anticipating. The full faith and credit clause (Article IV of the Constitution) requires one state to give full faith and credit to the laws and judicial orders of another state unless the laws or actions of the other state are against the public policy of the state asked to enforce them. Therefore, DOMA only provided for a state to do what the Constitution already empowered the state to do by virtue of the acknowledged exception to the full faith and credit clause. With or without DOMA, a state could still decline to recognize and enforce another state's same-sex marriage law by invoking the exception to the full faith and credit clause.

Windsor stands as a symbol of the Supreme Court's abandonment of judicial restraint and its transformation into a supreme legislature. This ruling undermines the legislative powers of Congress and the states, and it dismantles the balance of power that our founders put in the Constitution.

In another 5–4 case, *Hollingsworth v. Perry*, 570 U.S. 693 (2013), the Supreme Court struck down a major state referendum in California (Proposition 8) that would have limited marriage in that state to only heterosexual couples. This result was struck down on appeal, when the Supreme Court allowed the state of California to successfully appeal the referendum result to the California Supreme Court. But when the proponents for Proposition 8 appealed that ruling to the United States Supreme Court, that court ruled that the referendum proponents did not have standing to appeal. This ruling undermines the referendum processes in the twenty-seven state constitutions that provide for it.

These two cases demonstrate that a liberal political ideology took control of the Supreme Court, rejecting the principles of judicial restraint in order to establish a partisan, liberal ideology.

This abandonment of objective judicial standards turned the Supreme Court into a super legislature that can enact laws that Congress cannot or is unwilling to enact. This corruption of the Constitution can only be corrected by the President's nominating and the Senate's confirming only Justices who will set aside their political views and adhere to strict principles of judicial review. Currently, in America, it is only the Republicans who commit to do this. The Democrats specifically work to use the Court to establish their liberal views.

The control that the Democrat liberals achieved over the Supreme Court reached its pinnacle in the case of *Obergefell v. Hodges*, 576 U.S. ___ (2015), where the Supreme Court held that state laws that prohibit same-sex marriages are unconstitutional. Whether or not one agrees with the ultimate holding in *Obergefell*, what the Court did to reach its holding was atrocious, partisan, and was a rejection of principles of proper judicial review that had been a foundation of our law for more than two hundred years. In *Obergefell*, the Court employed the same approach it used in *Windsor*—it rejected the principle of judicial restraint and made false and negative aspersions on the intent of legislators of a law they didn't like. Then, in *Obergefell*, a slim liberal majority (five justices) established a wholly subjective standard for identifying nonenumerated rights. The Court again cited *Roe* as a basis for this. Chief Justice Roberts pointed out that this improper activism by the liberal justices undermines the constitutional rights and powers of Congress and the state legislatures and that the majority effectively reinstated the Supreme Court's flawed, subjective approach of the 1905 case of *Lochner v. New York*, 198 U.S. 45 (that was called "substantive due process")—which is nothing more than an exercise of imposing the political views of the Supreme Court in lieu of those of both Congress and state legislatures.

C. Federal Marriage Amendment Introduced

In May 2003, Colorado Republican Marilyn Musgrove introduced in the House of Representatives a proposed Federal Marriage Amendment (FMA). Subsequently, an identical amendment was proposed in the Senate. On February 24, 2004, President Bush announced his support for a FMA. Here is the wording of the amendment:

> Marriage in the United States shall consist only of the union of a man and a woman. Neither this Constitution or the constitution of any State, nor state or federal law, shall be construed to require that marital status or the legal incidents thereof be conferred upon unmarried couples or groups.[98]

At the time these FMA proposals were introduced, columnist Armstrong Williams reported that polls by the *New York Times,* CBS, *USA Today*, and CNN all found that more than 60 percent of Americans opposed legalizing homosexual unions.[99] But ten years later, that percentage dropped to 50 percent, or perhaps lower. In 2020, there does not seem to be any climate to either address or change the right of same-sex marriage that the Supreme Court established by judicial fiat in the *Obergefell* case of 2015.

While there is no current movement afoot to pass a constitutional amendment to permit only heterosexual marriages in America, it is nevertheless true that regulation of marriage is now substantially controlled by federal law. Beginning in 1965, in the landmark case of *Griswold v. Connecticut*, the Supreme Court began to take over regulating the rights and incidents of marriage. *Griswold* established

---

[98] As reported in the *Washington Times*, February 25, 2004.

[99] Armstrong Williams, "Marriage Rites and Civil Rights," the *Washington Times*, February 2004.

the right of married couples to use contraceptives. *Eisenstadt v. Baird* (1972) established the right of all adults to use contraceptives. And *Roe v. Wade* (1973) established the right of a woman to have an abortion. There is certainly some good in all of these cases, but they also represent significant limitations on what states can and cannot do to regulate marriages. The federal government has eventually taken over as a major supervisor and regulator of marriages in America.

It appears that the FMA has stalled and now lies dormant. It appears that half of America celebrates the new right to same-sex marriage, and that the other half has acquiesced in this change. If a majority of Americans wish to eliminate same-sex marriage, it would now require a constitutional amendment to do it.

CHAPTER SEVEN

The Frozen Embryo Custody Case

The Tennessee case of *Davis v. Davis*, 842 S.W.2d 588 (1992), brought out some interesting abortion-fetal rights questions that continue to be intriguing thirty years later. The facts leading up to this case began in the 1980s when a married couple, Junior Lewis Davis and Mary Sue Davis, tried unsuccessfully to have a child for several years; Mary Sue's fallopian tubes were damaged, preventing any fertilized egg from implanting in her womb. When the couple found that in vitro fertilization (IVF) presented a possible way to overcome the problem caused by the damaged fallopian tubes, they decided to try it.

By in vitro fertilization, eggs are surgically removed from the woman and are fertilized by the man's sperm in a laboratory dish. Later, the embryo, the fertilized egg, is implanted in a woman's womb, where it has an opportunity to grow and develop into a healthy, naturally delivered baby. That is the theory, and it has proven successful many times.

In the case of Mr. and Mrs. Davis, twelve eggs were fertilized and stored in a frozen condition—the embryos being preserved as miniscule entities, hardly visible. Later, five different attempts were made to implant one of the frozen embryos in Mrs. Davis. Each attempt was unsuccessful, and those embryos died in the process— leaving seven frozen embryos.

Then the situation hit a major legal snag when Mr. Davis filed for divorce on February 23, 1989, on the grounds of irreconcilable differences. The divorce worked out smoothly, except for deciding what was to become of the frozen seven. Mrs. Davis wanted custody of the embryos because she still wanted to have a baby, and being implanted with one of the seven embryos seemed to be her best chance to do so. But Mr. Davis did not want the responsibility of having to support any of the seven embryos if they should later become born children, subsequent to the divorce. Mrs. Davis said that she did not want any financial help from Mr. Davis if such a child were born. But legally, Mrs. Davis could not make a binding agreement that could be detrimental to her child. So the issue went to court.

A. The Trial

Mr. Davis was not seeking to have the embryos killed—he just didn't want to be responsible for up to seven children that could be brought into the world after the divorce—especially when he would be in a position of total helplessness as to if and when any of the embryos ever should be implanted in a womb and eventually born. Mr. Davis personally opposed abortion, but he took the position that conception does not occur until the embryo is implanted in the woman.

Some interesting testimony was given at the trial. Dr. I. Ray King, director of the IVF clinic, proposed that the embryos could be anonymously implanted in some other woman desirous of having a baby. Mr. and Mrs. Davis both opposed this. Dr. King pleaded with Judge W. Dale Young that no matter who wins, that the embryos not be destroyed. An expert witness from France also testified, pointing out that the imprint of a total and unique human being was already present with each of the embryos and that only the opportunity to mature and grow through pregnancy was needed for them to each develop into a new person. Dr. John Robertson, a law professor and an expert witness at the trial, called the frozen embryos "pre-embryos," to distinguish them from embryos that are naturally or artificially implanted in the uterus. Dr. Robertson argued that "since there are no state laws that say all pre-embryos must be implanted in the uterus, then a balance of burdens must be considered." He urged a "passive death" for the frozen embryos by thawing them.

After hearing the testimony and the legal and medical arguments, Judge Young took the case under advisement. About six weeks later, in September 1989, Judge Young issued his ruling: he gave Mrs. Davis custody of the embryos, ruling that this would be in "the best interest" of the pre-embryos. The judge postponed any ruling on child support until a later time. Mr. Davis appealed.[100]

B. Troubling Parts of the Judge's Ruling

Some of the legal issues that Judge Young grappled with had never before been addressed by a United States court. Because of this, the ruling has been studied and scrutinized for years.

The following are some areas of problem or concern that were raised by the *Davis* case and Judge Young's ruling.

1. *This ruling treated embryos as human beings rather than as potential human beings.* Never before had a court awarded custody of frozen embryos to someone. Previously, custody awards had always been reserved for live children. A logical extension of Judge Young's

---

[100] On appeal, Mr. Davis argued that the judge's ruling required him to be a parent against his will. The Tennessee appellate court agreed, and in 1990, it reversed the trial court. Mrs. Davis then appealed to the Tennessee Supreme Court, which affirmed the appellate court, *Davis v. Davis*, 842 S.W.2d 588 (1992). The Tennessee Supreme Court based its ruling on *Roe v. Wade*, which held that unborn fetuses are not "persons."

ruling would be that a court has the power to award custody of a fetus to someone other than the mother.

2. *Child support.* The one big issue that was necessarily postponed until another day is how much child support Mr. Davis would have to pay, when and if any or all of the seven embryos would mature into babies. Despite Judge Young's ruling, Mr. Davis had a good argument that the judge had no power to compel the payment of support payments in a case such as this where a couple is divorced prior to the wife's becoming pregnant.

3. *Judge Young discussed the right of pre-embryos to be brought to life* either through Mrs. Davis or through somebody else. "It is possible that the court might have them implanted in someone else," Judge Young wrote (according to one report). In fact, one commentator has suggested if the judge really meant what he said about pre-embryos' best interests in being brought to term through implantation, he would have had to order them implanted in someone else because Mrs. Davis had failed to carry the five embryos that were previously implanted in her. And who would the judge order to receive these seven "human beings" in need of a womb?

4. *Judge Young ruled that "human life" begins at conception* and that conception begins at the moment an egg is fertilized by a sperm, whether this occurs inside a woman or in a test tube. According to Judge Young's reasoning, Mrs. Davis conceived without becoming pregnant. This raises the question of whether our laws should distinguish between implanted embryos and embryos that are conceived and stored in a laboratory dish.

5. *Judge Young's ruling prohibited the killing of frozen embryos— even letting them passively die by thawing.* Even though *Roe v. Wade* established that a human fetus does not have a right to life, Judge Young ruled that the pre-embryos (pre-fetuses) did have a right to life. This inconsistency was obvious, and a year later, his ruling was overturned. But for a year, it put a duty on Tennessee IVF clinics not to allow leftover frozen embryos to die.

Judge Young made his ruling in the *Davis* case two and a half months following the Supreme Court abortion case of *Webster v. Reproductive Health Services*, 492 U.S. 490 (1989). The *Webster* case contained hints that four or five of the Supreme Court justices were considering protecting fetal life before it becomes viable (able to survive outside of the mother's womb). But how far back? In any event, as discussed previously (chapter 6), the Supreme Court never did extend a protection for fetal life to a time prior to viability.

6. *Should a state treat frozen pre-embryos like embryos that are living in a mother's womb?* What if our science and technology reach the point where a mechanical womb can be operated to grow and develop a pre-embryo, so that it can be born alive and survive without ever having to be in a woman? Shouldn't that pre-embryo life be protected just as much as normal embryonic life?

C. Suggested Principles to Apply to IVF

The frozen embryo custody case raises some delicate but powerful questions about how far our laws should go to protect fetal life. I believe that the overriding consideration in this debate should be a reverence for the sanctity of life. Technological practices and experiments that become mechanical and impersonal could lead to a disregard and desecration of the divine procreative processes involved. But the happy parents and families who have been blessed by this modern technology testify of the goodness that it has helped to bring to fruition in many cases. I would suggest that any laws regulating IVF activities should be family oriented, such that only lawfully married couples should be recipients of children brought about through the assistance of IVF.[101] Such a rule would have precluded Mrs. Davis from having any of the seven pre-embryos implanted in her unless she remarried or made other arrangements

---

[101] This will never happen in the current legal environment, where adoptions are routinely finalized for both single parents and for same-sex partners.

for the care of her "pre-children." A simplified adoption procedure for pre-embryos could be made to allow them to be placed with a couple to parent the future child. Another suggestion is that only a limited number of eggs should be allowed to be fertilized at a time, rather than fertilizing and stockpiling many pre-embryos.

CHAPTER EIGHT

The Right Not to Be Conceived

Park v. Chessin, 387 N.Y.S.2d 204 (1976)

Lara Park was born with polycystic kidney disease, a congenital disease. She lived for two and a half years before dying of this disease. During her life, she suffered great pain from this birth defect. Previous to Lara's birth, her mother had given birth to another child who also had polycystic kidney disease and who died shortly after birth. The doctors, who treated Mrs. Park during both pregnancies, did not inform her after the first child's birth that polycystic kidney disease was hereditary in nature and that if she had other children, they would probably suffer from this same disease.

Mr. and Mrs. Park then had another child, Lara, not anticipating having a similar problem with her. After Lara's death, the parents brought an action on behalf of the child[102] against the doctors for negligence in failing to inform them of the hereditary nature of their first child's disease and of the likelihood of subsequent children also having the same disease. The parents claimed that the doctors' negligence induced them to have another child that they otherwise

---

[102] The parents also brought several actions in their own behalf, which are not pertinent to this discussion.

would not have had. The parents, on behalf of Lara, sought damages for the conscious pain and suffering that Lara had as a result of her congenital birth defect.

The court was faced with the following issue: does there exist after birth a legal right to make a claim for pain and suffering resulting from a tort committed prior to conception?[103] The court held that such a claim stated a valid cause of action and denied the defendants' motion for dismissal.

These facts describe the New York State court case of *Park v. Chessin* 387 N.Y.S.2d 204 (1976). (The ruling was upheld on appeal, 60 A.D.2d 80 [1977].) The issue before that court was one of first impression, as it would have been in most jurisdictions. This case is significant for two reasons. First, it extends fetal rights to an extreme never before recognized in the law. Never before have courts allowed causes of action to be brought for torts committed prior to conception. As will be seen in this discussion, the New York court recognized a right not to be conceived.[104] Second, this case magnifies a continuing inconsistency in the area of fetal rights, stemming from the *Roe v. Wade* decision. Briefly stated, that inconsistency is that unborn children are recognized as having some rights, such as in the areas of property law and torts, but not the right to life itself. The implications of the *Park v. Chessin* case dramatically point out the tragic inequity of this inconsistency.

The purpose of this chapter is twofold: (1) to examine the validity of *Park v. Chessin* decision, and regardless of the outcome of the examination, (2) to show how this case accentuates the inconsistency

---

[103]   387 N.Y.S.2d at 205–206.

[104]   What basis is there for the right not to be conceived? Such a right, if it does exist, either must (1) reside in some nonmortal being who would later inhabit the body, or (2) the body itself must have a right to be other than it is. As to the former, we can only second guess what the spirit being would want. Perhaps it, or God, has the power to determine whether a particular spirit will inhabit a particular body. The latter possibility is absurd. If the deformed body itself is the source of a right, then how could it possibly have acquired a right to be other than it is?

in giving children the right to enjoy a certain quality of life after birth but at the same time not giving children the right to be born alive. Until either all fetal rights are abolished or the fetal right to life is recognized, a double standard will continue to govern the area of fetal rights.

A. Background

Fetal rights developed gradually in the nineteenth and twentieth centuries. One of the first recognized rights of a fetus was the right to an inheritance. This right was contingent upon the fetus's live birth. Judges began to be troubled, however, by the double standard that existed by recognizing inheritance and property rights for the unborn but not recognizing the right of an unborn child to recover for tortious physical injury.[105] In response to this inconsistency, various jurisdictions began to allow prenatal personal injury actions if the child was viable at the time of the injury and if it survived birth.[106] Gradually, the requirement that the child be viable at the time of the injury was abandoned. Now children are often allowed to bring claims whether or not they were viable when the injury occurred.[107] Now, too, in many jurisdictions, stillborn babies are permitted to recover for injuries suffered as viable fetuses.[108] In *Zepeda v. Zepeda,* an Illinois court suggested that a child might be able to recover for a tort committed before conception:

---

[105] *Zepeda v. Zepeda*, 41 Ill.App.2d 240, 248-249, 190 N.E.2d 849, 850.

[106] *Id.*

[107] *Id.; Kelley v. Gregory*, 282 App. Div. 542, 125 N.Y.S.2d 696 (N.Y. Sup. Ct. 1953). *Kelly v. Gregory* was the first case to expressly reject viability as the starting point where the rights of the unborn child begin. The court moved the point back because biological knowledge demonstrated that separate biological life exists from the moment of conception (282 App. Div. at 543–544).

[108] In 1977, seventeen states allowed stillborn babies to recover for injuries suffered as viable fetuses, fifteen did not. See footnote 25, above.

[I]f recovery is to be permitted an infant injured
one month after conception, why not if injured
one week after, one minute after, or at the moment
of conception? It is inevitable that the date will be
further retrogressed .... If there is human life, proved
by subsequent birth, then that human life has the
same rights at the time of conception as it has at any
time thereafter .... But what if the wrongful conduct
takes place before conception? Can the defendant be
held accountable if his act was completed before the
plaintiff was conceived? Yes, for it is possible to incur,
as Justice Holmes phrased it in the Dietrich case,[109] "a
conditional prospective liability in tort to one not yet
in being .... It makes no difference how much time
elapses between a wrongful act and a resulting injury
if there is a causal relationship between them.[110]

In *Piper v. Hoard*, 107 N.Y. 73, 13 N.E. 626, a New York court enforced
an inheritance right that was created prior to conception. In that case, the
defendant fraudulently represented that if the plaintiff's mother would
marry, her heir would have a certain farm. This promise induced the
mother to marry. But when the plaintiff was born to her, the defendant
reneged. The court, however, held the defendant to his representation
and gave the farm to the plaintiff, heir. The fetal inheritance right in
Piper v. Hoard existed before conception. But should a claim for personal
injuries be upheld where the tort was committed before conception?
Prior to *Park v. Chessin*, two New York cases touched on this issue:
Howard v. Lecher, 386 N.Y.S.2d 460 (App. Div., 2d Dept. 1976); and *Stewart
v. Long Is. Coll. Hosp.*, 35 A.D.2d 531, 313 N.Y.S.2d 502, aff'd. 30 N.Y.2d
695, 332 N.Y.S.2d 640, 283 N.E.2d 616 (App. Div., 2d Dept.).

---

[109] *Dietrich v. Inhabitants of Northampton*, 138 Mass. 14 (1884).

[110] 41 Ill. App. 2d 248–249. See also *Endresz v. Friedberg*, 24 N.Y.S.2d 478, 485–486, 301
N.Y.S.2d 65, 70 248 N.E.2d 901, 904.

In *Howard v. Lecher*, a child's parents brought an action claiming damages for "their own" mental distress and emotional disturbance allegedly resulting from their daughter's suffering and dying from Tay-Sachs, a fatal genetic disorder. The parents claimed that the obstetrician and gynecologist knew, or should have known, that they were potential carriers of Tay-Sachs disease and that defendants failed to properly test and advise them to alert them of the possibility of having a diseased child. The parents contended that the child had a right not to be born and that had they been advised that the fetus had the disease, they would have procured a legal abortion. The court dismissed the claim stating that "[s]uits seeking recovery of damages due solely to the existence of life (having been born alive) or 'wrongful life,' rather than no life, had not met favor with the courts."

In *Stewart v. Long Is. Coll. Hosp.*, the same court that had earlier decided *Howard* dealt with an action brought by the parents on behalf of an infant, suing the hospital for failing to do an abortion and thereby terminate the infant's fetal life. The child had been born with birth defects that caused her serious physical and mental disabilities that could never be corrected. The parents alleged that the hospital knew that the child would be born with these severe disabilities and that the hospital was negligent by refusing to abort the baby. Eventually, the appellate court dismissed this action, holding that such a cause of action was unknown to the law and would not be entertained until it became sanctioned by legislation.

B. The Instant Case

In *Park v. Chessin*, the court set out the development of prenatal rights in tort law among much the same lines as discussed above. The court said that both *Howard* and *Stewart* were distinguishable and allowed the child to recover for a wrong committed before the child was conceived.

The court first said that *Howard* differed from the instant case in two ways. First, *Howard* did not deal with the issue of whether a child could recover for being born diseased but rather whether the parents could recover for the mental distress that the child's birth defects caused them to suffer. Second, the tort in *Howard*, though similar to that in *Park v. Chessin*, occurred after the child had already been conceived. In *Howard*, the doctor's malpractice did not influence the couple to become pregnant, as in the instant case. Furthermore, in that case, the parents claimed that had they known the baby had Tay-Sachs disease, they would have aborted the child for the sake of the child. The court, however, was not willing to recognize a right not to be conceived and not to be born.

The court distinguished *Stewart* by pointing out that whereas *Stewart* sought to create a fetal right to not have life ("wrongful life"), the *Park v. Chessin* case was an action to recover damages for pain and suffering rather than to recover damages for being conceived and born.

Satisfied that it had distinguished these two cases, the court then went on to extend the right to recover for prenatal personal injuries to include the right to recover for torts committed before conception where the child is subsequently born alive.

C. Analysis

1. <u>Did the court correctly distinguish *Howard* and *Stewart*?</u> A closer examination of both *Howard* and *Stewart* reveals that neither of them were correctly distinguished. The *Park v. Chessin* holding is contrary to both of these prior decisions.

Although it is true that in *Howard* the action was brought on behalf of the parents, rather than on behalf of the child, the court's language in *Howard* clearly indicated that a child could not bring an action for being wrongfully given life. The *Park v. Chessin* court correctly distinguished the cases on their facts but clearly disregarded the *Howard* court's reasoning, where the court had said it would not recognize a claim for "wrongful life."

The court distinguished *Stewart* by saying that in that case, the child sought to enforce a right not to be born, whereas in *Park v. Chessin*, the child only sought to recover damages for the pain and suffering experienced after being born. While this seems reasonable at first, it is quite clearly a meaningless distinction. This distinction implies that the doctors could have avoided liability by not causing the injury and at the same time letting the child be conceived and live. But, of course, this is an impossibility. There was no way to alleviate the congenital kidney disease and also allow the child to live. The only way to prevent the disease was to prevent or terminate the child's life. The only way to have prevented the child's pain and suffering was to prevent the child from being conceived and born. Therefore, *Park* is not distinguishable from *Stewart*. *Stewart* should have been controlling.

By trying to make this distinction, the court was much more creative than the plaintiff had been. In fact, the plaintiffs' pleadings were made in the exact same terms that were explicitly rejected in *Stewart*. The plaintiffs claimed that the child had a right not to be conceived and not to be born. The plaintiffs argued that this right was their basis for recovering damages for pain and suffering. The plaintiffs realized that these two aspects of their claim were indistinguishable. The court, however, failed to connect the two.

Although the court in *Park* said it was not recognizing a right not to be conceived and not to live, that is the precise effect of the holding. The court's attempted distinction exists merely in the realm of word structure and not in the real world of logic.

2. *Hypothetical—a cause of action against the mother.* The following hypothetical illustrates a serious potential problem that would result by permitting tort claims to arise before conception: Suppose that the prospective parents learned that if they were to

have children, their children would probably be born with serious congenital deformities. In spite of this knowledge, they decide to have a child anyway. A child is then conceived, and it does have a serious congenital problem. The mother refuses to have an abortion because of her religious convictions. Furthermore, she believes that despite the severe and painful handicap that the child would have, that the spirit inside the child would still prefer to be born alive than to be aborted. After the wife becomes pregnant, suppose the husband changes his mind and now does not want the child to be born and have to suffer. The mother still refuses to have an abortion. Eventually the child is born with serious and painful birth defects, and the father sues the mother on behalf of the child for all the pain and suffering that the child experiences.[111] Can the child recover against the mother?

The only difference from this hypothetical and the factual situation in *Park v. Chessin* is a difference in who committed the tort. From the child's point of view, nothing has changed. And yet in this hypothetical, the child would be prevented from recovering under *Roe v. Wade* (a woman's right to control her body and to have an abortion)[112] and *Eisenstadt v. Baird* (an individual's right to bear and beget a child).

It is only logical that if the child can recover from the doctor,

---

[111] Although some interesting standing issues could be raised here, none of them are really valid because the suit is being brought on behalf of the child. If the father would not bring such an action, perhaps the state could bring such an action, or if the child survives, he or she could bring such an action.

[112] In *Roe v. Wade* the Supreme Court attempted to resolve the abortion question without answering the fundamental issue of when fetal life begins. The Court said that it "need not resolve the difficult question of when life begins," 410 U.S. at 159, and yet the effect of *Roe* is to establish that the right to life does not exist until birth. The Court did say that if it could be established that a fetus is a "person" within the meaning of the Fourteenth Amendment, then abortion could be constitutionally prohibited. But the Court could find no such right. The Court failed to acknowledge the laws in seventeen states that provided wrongful death actions for stillborn babies. (See footnote 25, above.) Whether these statutes were intended to be invalidated by *Roe* was not explicitly stated. It would seem

then the child should be able to recover from the parent as well. From the child's point of view, it makes no difference. But the child could not recover from the mother. This means that the existence of the child's cause of action depends upon who inflicts the tort and not solely upon whether the victim is injured. If it is the child that the law seeks to protect, then the child should be able to recover against the parents as well as the doctor.

I would have predicted that *Park v. Chessin* would be overturned. But it was upheld on appeal the next year (60 A.D.2d 80 [1977]). Therefore, the conflict continues. On the one hand, a fetus has a right to be born having certain physical qualities, but on the other hand, the fetus does not have a right to be born. The real problem with this inconsistency is that it is not there by accident. There are two main rationales used to defend it. One is the contingency fiction, which states that the fetus actually has no rights until it is born alive.[113] The flaw in this explanation is that the contingency was not created to prevent a fetus from later recovering but rather was created because until the child is born it is not capable of recovering anything.[114] This contingency was not intended to prevent future recovery, and yet it

---

that if criminal antiabortion statutes are invalid, many of the wrongful death statutes for stillborn babies would also be invalid.

[113] 387 N.Y.S.2d at 210; *Endresz, supra*, at 483, 485–486; *Keyes v. Construction Serv.*, 340 Mass. 633, 636, 165 N.E.2d 912, 915; see also Hopkins, supra at 720.

[114] The contingency provisions in statutes providing prenatal tort actions should not be construed to mean that an unborn fetus possesses no rights. An equally plausible interpretation of this contingency, in fact an interpretation that is actually much more plausible, is that the contingency merely goes to the question of standing. A common standing provision is to provide that no tort actions will be allowed where the victim does not survive to bring the action and recover in person. It is felt that if they are not alive to bring the action, entertaining such an action would require the tortfeasor to compensate someone incapable of being compensated. Such an action would be a penal action. As a matter of public policy, a state might not wish to allow such actions.

The contingency of fetal rights was never intended to be used to extinguish other fetal rights. But this is exactly what the Court used the contingency to accomplish in *Roe*. The Court should have realized that the contingency of live birth was not created to be used to extinguish other rights.

has been used to deny fetuses the right to live. The second rationale acknowledges the inconsistency and says it is just and fair; it merely restates the inconsistency as a positive good: if a child is born, it has a right not to suffer from any pain or from any physical or mental deformities, but it does not have a right to be born. If anything, the rationale goes, it has a right not to be born with deformities.

This second viewpoint has three main weaknesses. First, it fails to acknowledge that the right to life is "the right to have rights."[115] This view entails the guarantee of a certain quality of life while at the same time saying that the existing life itself has no right to continue existing. If a fetus has no right to live, then it is irrational to protect its right to a certain quality of life. The second weakness in this viewpoint is a corollary to the first; that is, in setting a minimum quality of life standard that all born children have a right to have. Who can say what characteristics a person has a right to be born with? Does a person have a right to be born if he or she would be a diabetic, have a deformed limb, or be mentally impaired in some degree? If so, to what degree? We should not forget Hitler's atrocities with eugenics—in attempting to eliminate those that he felt did not meet his minimal standards. Who is competent to draw such lines? The third weakness with this view is that the solution it calls for to prevent birth defects is to kill defective fetuses, rather than to eliminate the disease without killing the individual. It is interesting to note, in this respect, that research is presently being done to attempt to eliminate congenital birth defects both in fetuses and in the parent carriers.[116]

Park v. Chessin symbolizes the inconsistency of giving a child the right to a certain quality of life after birth but not giving the child a right to be born. *Park v. Chessin* is a symbol of this inconsistency. As

---

[115] *Furman v. Georgia* (death penalty case).

[116] The National Institutes of Health is currently (and has been since the 1970s) doing research with DNA (the basic building block of human genes). Dr. Donald Frederickson testified to a House subcommittee in 1977 that the benefits of this research could be enormous. UPI Press Release, Provo *Daily Herald*, March 20, 1977, p. 20.

was said at the outset, the problem will continue to exist unless and until either the fetal right to life is established or other fetal rights are extinguished.

D. Conclusion

The *Park v. Chessin* case was erroneously decided. The court was mistaken in thinking it could allow a child to recover damages for pain and suffering and not allow a child to recover for having been wrongfully conceived and wrongfully allowed to live and be born. Where the injury suffered is inseparably connected with life itself, by allowing the child to recover for the wrongful injury, the court also, necessarily, allowed the child to recover for wrongful life.

Park v. Chessin illustrates the present inconsistency in fetal rights: A fetus may later recover for minor injuries that do not prevent birth, but a fetus has no right to recover for a major injury that causes its death (because a fetus is not recognized as having a right to live). Although the Supreme Court may excuse itself in this, by saying that all fetal rights are contingent upon live birth and therefore do not really exist until birth, this legal fiction defies logic. If logic and common sense were the important considerations, there would be no need for the contingency fiction. Until either the fetal right to life is again established (this time explicitly in the Constitution) or all other fetal rights are abolished, this confusing inconsistency will continue to plague the equitable administration of justice in the area of fetal rights.

CHAPTER NINE

The Bogeyman

Webster defines a *bogeyman* as "an imaginary frightful being, esp. one used as a threat to children in disciplining them."[117] *Roe v. Wade* is a bogeyman to the pro-choicers. If someone even mentions the thought of reversing or modifying *Roe v. Wade*, the proabortion crowd goes into hysteria where they cannot see straight—and they rail emotionally against anyone who dares criticize *Roe*. During the last forty-seven years, by invoking this hysteria, the abortion lovers have been extremely successful in causing many pro-lifers to back off, hide, shut up, and avoid conflict and controversy. I expect the bogeyman phenomenon to continue to be employed by the pro-choicers as long as it continues to work.

As long as pro-lifers are intimidated by the antics of the pro-choicers, then even a majority of pro-lifers will be kept at bay, America will continue to have eight hundred thousand abortions every year, and there will be no right-to-life amendment. The political successes of both Ronald Reagan and Donald Trump show that half of America, if not more, opposes abortion except to save the mother or in cases of rape or incest. America can enact a fetal right-to-life amendment if we have the courage to publicly take a stand on this issue.

---

[117] *Webster's New World Dictionary of the American Language*, Second College Edition (William Collins + World Publishing Co., Inc., 1978).

From 1973 until today, a vocal segment of America has celebrated the *Roe* case and campaigned ferociously against anyone who has dared to criticize the absolute right to an abortion.[118] But it is certainly worth noting that while the pro-choice lobby insists that the right to have an abortion is the foundation of their liberty, they do not like to refer to this as being proabortion. They have a slew of euphemisms that they use instead: "reproductive freedom," "reproductive health," "a woman's right to control her own body," "terminating a pregnancy," "freedom of choice," "a procedure," "family planning," "access to health care," and "choice." The consistent use of these euphemisms shows that even they are uncomfortable with the gruesome procedure that terminates human life.

As people become better informed about abortion, many of them come to realize that unborn human babies do have the right to live. Two polls on abortion that demonstrated this were the 1972 voting results in Michigan and North Dakota, where the citizens voted directly on legalized abortion. Both proabortion and pro-life forces conducted extensive educational campaigns. Michigan voted no on abortion by 62 percent, and North Dakota voted no on abortion by 78 percent.[119] These results confirmed the fact that the more people become informed about abortion, the greater their opposition was to legalized abortion.[120]

---

[118] Probably the most powerful organization that supports abortion is NARAL Pro-Choice America (or NARAL, for short). NARAL was founded in 1969 and is the oldest abortion rights advocacy group in America. Initially, it was called the National Association for the Repeal of Abortion Laws. Following the *Roe v. Wade* ruling in 1973, they changed the name to National Abortion Rights Action League. NARAL continues to lobby for candidates and laws that are proabortion.

[119] North Dakota was only 12 percent Catholic. Michigan had 51 percent of its people "unchurched," and preelection polls had shown that over 60 percent were proabortion (*Handbook*, p. 36). It is interesting to note that subsequent to *Roe*, twenty state legislatures passed resolutions to inform Congress that they condemned the Court's abortion decision. Initially, no state formally approved the decision (*Handbook*, p. 160).

[120] The "Congressional Quarterly" of August 28, 1976, pages 2344–2345, reported that the "[s]entiment on the abortion issue has shifted dramatically in the last two years." In

In 1977, most Americans personally opposed abortion except to save the life of the mother. This was clearly demonstrated by congressional voting on tax-funded abortions in 1976 and 1977. Nevertheless, there were many public polls circulating then that misrepresented this fact. A Gallup Poll in November 1974 reported that 52 percent of those polled agreed that abortions through the third month of pregnancy should continue to be legal, while 48 percent disagreed.[121] Most polls on abortion, like this one, did not ask whether one personally disapproves of abortion but whether they believe women who do want abortions should be allowed to have them. This points out one of the greatest obstacles to the passage of a right-to-life amendment: though people personally oppose abortion, they are reluctant to impose this standard on others. This reasoning, however, fails to recognize that those who participate in an abortion impose on an unborn child their own determination of whether or not that child deserves to live.

In the more than four decades after *Roe*, about half of the nation—maybe more—has continued to be critical of *Roe*. In 1980, Ronald Reagan was a pro-life candidate, and this helped rather than hurt his candidacy. In 1989, the Supreme Court was one justice shy of overturning *Roe*, in the case of *Webster v. Reproductive Health Services*, 492 U.S. 490. In 2000, a *Los Angeles Times* poll reported that 65 percent of respondents said abortion should be illegal after the first trimester. Interestingly, more women (72 percent) thought it

---

1974, the House easily rejected, 123–247, an amendment that would bar the use of any federal funds for abortion. The Senate passed such an amendment, but the bill died in conference. In 1976, the House passed such an amendment, but the Senate defeated it. In 1976, however, the Ninety-Fourth Congress's joint conference committee agreed to a compromise that kept the amendment alive, and it was finally passed, providing that no federal funds were to be used to pay for abortions "except where the life of the mother would be endangered if the fetus were carried to term." "Congressional Quarterly," September 18, 1976, p. 2541.

[121] The United States Commission on Civil Rights, "Constitutional Aspects of the Right to Limit Childbearing," Washington, DC, 1975, p. 82.

should be illegal than men (58 percent).[122] Women oppose abortion more than men.

A. The 2008 Presidential Election Campaign

No president has ever had a more radical, offensive stance on abortion than Barack Obama. His support of abortion was so extreme that as an Illinois state senator, he blocked legislation that would require the participating parties to attempt to save the lives of children who were born alive after failed abortions. This is a barbaric and reprehensible position.

In 2008, the selection of Sarah Palin as the Republican vice presidential nominee was a home run for the Republican nominee, Senator John McCain. She was a true conservative. She wanted to drill for oil in Alaska, where she was governor. Not only did she say that she was pro-family, but she had a large family to prove it. Not only did she say she was pro-life, but she loved the Down's syndrome baby that she bore at age forty-four, five months earlier. She was attractive and articulate. She was proud of her small-town roots. She challenged the man-made global warming alarmists. She despised the politically correct, left wing mantras. She did for the Republican Party what John McCain could not do—energized the conservative base. Both Senator McCain and Governor Palin were solidly for the right to life—and starkly opposed the Democratic ticket's proabortion stance. Sarah Palin's nomination initially catapulted the McCain/Palin ticket ahead of Obama/Biden in the polls.

That was not good for Senators Obama and Biden. They were desperate to stop the McCain/Palin Express before they got run over. This called for an early deployment of the Democrats' ace card—the *Roe v. Wade* bogeyman ad tactic! The Democrats may have preferred to wait until later in the campaign to play this card, but the explosive

---

[122] Reported in Ann Coulter, *Godless—The Church of Liberalism* (New York: Crown Publishing Group, 2006), p. 91.

success of Sarah Palin had precipitated the Democrats' plunge in the polls and had put them into panic mode. Then, on September 5, 2008, on the way home from work, I heard on the radio three times a new ad from Senator Obama—the ad warned the women of America that McCain would overturn *Roe v. Wade* and that this would endanger the health of American women and deprive them of their cherished right to an abortion.

Ultimately, President Obama prevailed in the 2008 election. I don't believe abortion was the major issue in this contest, but the bogeyman ad did seem to help.

B. The 2012 Presidential Election Campaign

Move forward to 2012, when President Obama was running for reelection, and he continued to support a woman's absolute right to an abortion. During the campaign, in mid-August 2012, the nation focused on a strange statement made by Rep. Todd Akin (R-MO), when he said that in cases of "legitimate" rape, the woman's body has a way to take care of itself. Democrats triumphantly broadcast Akin's gaff for a week and used this as a way to paint Republicans as being ignorant and antiwomen. Although the pro-choice/pro-life debate was not a central part of this presidential contest, it seemed that pro-choicers were in the majority. President Obama won reelection by defeating challenger Mitt Romney.

C. The 2016 and 2020 Presidential Election Campaigns

In 2016, the Republican presidential nominee Donald Trump campaigned boldly as a pro-life candidate; he expressed dissatisfaction with *Roe v. Wade*; and he spoke out strongly against partial-birth abortion as being cruel and inhumane. By taking this position,

Donald Trump disputed the conventional wisdom that doing so would hurt him at the polls. Nevertheless, he did it, and he was elected president. He was the strongest pro-life presidential candidate since Ronald Reagan. Trump's victory is an indication that half of America likely approved of his position of opposing abortion except as necessary to protect the life of the mother or in cases rape or incest. It appears that the proabortion forces are not as numerous as they would like people to think. There may yet be sufficient support among American voters to recognize a fetal right to life.

In 2020, President Donald Trump continued to be pro-life. In January of this year, he attended and spoke at the annual pro-life rally in Washington, DC, that draws thousands of supporters each year to protest against the Supreme Court's *Roe v. Wade* decision of January 22, 1973. Trump is the first president of the United States to ever personally attend this annual event. President Trump's political opponent celebrates *Roe v. Wade* and attempts to use Trump's pro-life position as a reason to vote against him. But I'm not sure that this issue will hurt Trump. A majority support prohibiting partial-birth abortion. Perhaps a majority of Americans would now support a fetal right-to-life amendment.

D. Confronting the Bogeyman

But the bogeyman stands in the way. No Supreme Court case has been more of a lightning rod for polarizing political debate than the *Roe v. Wade* decision. That case was controversial from the moment it was announced, and it has remained controversial ever since. Every time a president nominates a new Justice for the Supreme Court, the most important question for interrogation is whether or not that nominee would overturn *Roe v. Wade*. But rather than addressing the *Roe v. Wade* issues seriously, the three-second sound bite answers provide no in-depth discussion of this issue. Let me share insights about four specific issues pertaining to reversing *Roe v. Wade*.

1. *Reversing* Roe *would not necessarily eliminate a woman's right to privacy.* If *Roe v. Wade* ever were reversed or overturned, there are several ways in which it could happen—none of which would require eliminating a woman's right to privacy and of control over her own body. These alternatives would limit a woman's right but not extinguish it.

2. Roe v. Wade *allowed Congress and the states to prohibit partial-birth abortion.* As terrible as *Roe v. Wade* was in 1973, it did allow states to prohibit late-term abortions, including partial-birth abortions. Partial-birth abortion literally kills a viable fetus by crushing its skull and sucking its brains out. In 2003, Congress did pass the Partial Birth Abortion Ban Act, which prohibits such abortions, except if necessary to save the life of the mother. (The Supreme Court upheld this law in *Gonzalez v. Carhart*, 550 U.S. 124 [2007].)

3. *A president can neither overturn a case nor amend the Constitution.* Contrary to the assertion in the 2008 Obama ad, the president of the United States cannot overturn *Roe v. Wade*. That can happen only by the Supreme Court reversing itself or by passage of a constitutional amendment, the latter of which can only be done by the consensus of a supermajority—that is, the approval of three-quarters of the states. The president has no role in this.

4. *Part of* Roe v. Wade *is good—recognizing a woman's right to privacy.* The idea that every part of *Roe v. Wade* could be or would be overturned is ridiculous. Remember, *Roe v. Wade* is a very complex case. I don't ever recall a serious public discussion about what part of *Roe v. Wade* one would or would not want to overturn. The woman's right to privacy—the right to control her own body—that will never be overturned. That part of *Roe v. Wade* is laudable. But it would be good for the law to acknowledge the existence of a fetal right to continue living that would have to be weighed against a woman's right to control her body. Extinguishing the fetal right to life was the most opprobrious part of *Roe v. Wade*. It should be restored, and such a restoration would mean that the right to an abortion would not be

an absolute; it would have to be weighed against the fetal right to life. In summary, if *Roe v. Wade* ever were "overturned," it would only be one or two aspects of that ruling that would be changed. Possible changes could include (a) returning the abortion issue to the states; (b) restoring the fetal right to life; and/or (c) correcting the ruling that a fetus is not a person.

The discussion about which parts of *Roe v. Wade* should be overturned and which should remain would be an important discussion. I welcome it. Parts of *Roe v. Wade* should be overturned. But those who cling to abortion as the sacrament of their political religion—they don't want the discussion.

There are multiple types of support for the right to life. But not all right-to-lifers have the same beliefs and principles about whether abortions are ever justified and about what conditions might justify an abortion. In the rare instances where abortion would preserve a mother's life, a large majority would find it acceptable. It may also be proper in the case of certain severely deformed babies. And a majority would also support abortion in cases of rape or incest—because in those cases, a pregnancy was forced upon a woman against her will. Extinguishing a fetal right to life does simplify the administration of the law—but it is cruel and barbaric. Correcting this serious flaw would require overturning part of *Roe v. Wade*. But that's okay—it would be an improvement. But pro-life people will have to face and deal with the bogeyman first. Good people will have to have the courage and resolve and determination to go through ridicule, threats, derision, and hostility in order to succeed.

Drawing the fine lines as to when an abortion might be appropriate and legal and when it should be prohibited or limited in order to protect fetal life will never satisfy everyone. There must be an acknowledgment that there are some instances, even though they may be only a few, when an abortion would be justified. But the total disregard for the sanctity and preciousness of developing human life in the mother is a grievous moral deficiency in our laws. The value of each and every independent human life should be recognized. It is not too late to reestablish a fetal right to life. The current state of our laws—that disregards human life before birth—is an abomination. We have a duty to amend our laws to correct this.

CHAPTER TEN

Legislating Morality

One obstacle facing the right-to-life position is the feeling by some people that morality should not be legislated. Some contend that people do not have the right to impose their moral standards on others. Frankly, this point of view is shallow, uninformed, illogical, and naive. Every law imposes someone's moral standards on others. It is impossible for a law not to impose somebody's moral standards. The only question is, Whose moral standards will be imposed? And in a democratic republic, the answer is the standards of a majority of the people.

During oral argument before the Supreme Court on a case involving tax-funded abortions, the UPI reported the following exchange that occurred:

> Justice William Rehnquist asked what is wrong constitutionally about legislating for a moral reason. Walsh [counsel for one of the parties] said lawmakers would be imposing their view on the populace. "Isn't that the purpose of any legislation?" asked Rehnquist. "Presumably it represents the views of the populace," [Justice] Stewart cut in.[123]

---

[123] UPI wire report, Provo *Daily Herald*, January 13, 1977, p. 45.

Attorney Brian H. Kelley made the following succinct comments on this matter:

> The question is not whether or not we should enforce morals, but rather, which morals we shall enforce. And perhaps a second question, whose morals should we enforce. As society tries to make distinctions between "political" crimes and "moral" crimes, we cannot make such distinctions. We have no choice. Morals are legislated.[124]

Brian Kelley also addressed the situation where some laws remain on our books, even though they are rarely enforced (e.g., laws making adultery a crime). Mr. Kelley offered the following:

> There may be two additional reasons to keep laws on the books even in the face of disobedience. While laws may not be effective in prohibiting certain conduct, they imply that society does not condone such activity. Lastly, perhaps certain laws should remain on the books simply to preserve the integrity of society, to stand as a witness that [such] activities are ... not in accordance with God's laws or with the laws of the land.[125]

The existence of freedom does not require or imply the absence of all laws. Rather, the very existence of laws has been required because some people have abused the rights of others. Laws have then been passed and enforced to protect people from being hurt and abused by others. With regard to protecting unborn humans

---

[124] Brian H. Kelley, "On Legislating Morality," unpublished paper, October 19, 1976, p. 3.

[125] *Id.*, 2–3.

from unwarranted killings, a fetal right-to-life amendment is now needed.

The Church of Jesus Christ of Latter-day Saints has this belief about the rights and obligations of people to make and uphold good laws: "We believe that governments were instituted of God for the benefit of man; and that he holds men accountable for their acts in relation to them, both in making laws and administering them, for the good and safety of society" (*Doctrine and Covenants*, 134:1). Citizens are responsible to make good laws. God will hold them responsible for the laws they make as well as for the laws they do not make that they should have made. (See, for example, *Doctrine and Covenants*, 98:4–7). Elder Ezra Taft Benson (as president of the Quorum of the Twelve) said in 1976:

> A citizen of this republic cannot do his duty and be an idle spectator. How appropriate and vital it is at this time of our nation's 200th birthday to remember this counsel from the Lord: "Honest men and wise men should be sought for diligently, and good men and wise men ye should observe to uphold" (D&C 98:10). Wise and honorable men raised that glorious standard for this nation. It will also take wise and honorable men to perpetuate what was so nobly established.[126]

To summarize, someone's morality is always involved in the making of laws. It is right and proper to establish laws that help protect some people from those who would harm or kill them. Laws that prescribe sanctions for violators do not necessarily violate a person's free agency; individuals may choose whether or not to obey the law and whether or not to subject themselves to the consequences

---

[126] *Ensign*, May 1976, pp. 92–93.

of breaking that law. Thus, people are free to choose either liberty through obedience or captivity through violating the law.[127]

In conclusion, it is not only right and proper, but it is of critical importance that God-fearing people attempt to correct flaws in our laws that contribute to the warrantless killing of unborn human life. Passage of a fetal right-to-life amendment would help preserve the life of the defenseless human beings whose lives have been extinguished at the rate of over a million a year in America since the *Roe v. Wade* decision was announced in 1973.[128]

The right of human fetuses to live was recognized in most states in America before 1973. In 1973, the United States Supreme Court in *Roe v. Wade* held that a fetus has no right to life and is not a "person" within the meaning of the due process clause of the Fourteenth Amendment. This part of the *Roe v. Wade* holding is terrible! It is disgusting! And it is an afront to God. We must never forget the egregious wrongs done by the Supreme Court in this case. If we can pass a fetal right-to-life amendment—even now, forty-seven years after the court ruled in *Roe*—then we should. Passage of such an amendment would not eliminate that part of *Roe* that recognizes that a woman has a right to privacy that gives her important rights over her body, including pertaining to human life within her when she is pregnant. A proper resolution of the ongoing problem—the problem that was made worse by *Roe v. Wade*—is that a fetal right to life should be recognized in our law, and it should be balanced with a woman's right to control her body when the two rights come into conflict.

---

[127] *Book of Mormon*, 2 Nephi 2:26–27.

[128] The Guttmacher Institute reports that from 1973 to 2018, there have been 61,628,584 abortions in the US (about 1.35 million/year). The Center for Disease Control (CDC) reports approximately forty-five million abortions in America through 2015, but the CDC totals do not include numbers from the state of California and some other states. There has been a gradual decline in abortions in the US, beginning in 1998. The number of abortions reported by Guttmacher for 2017 is 862,320. See the NRLC website, "Abortion Statistics." See https://nrlc.org/uploads/factsheets/FS01AbortionintheUS.

Whether or not we can ever correct our laws to protect precious, independent human life that nestles in a mother's womb—I do not know. If we can protect it, we should. If we can't, then at the very least, we should recognize the serious flaw in our laws that treat the most precious and special human beings as worthless dross.

We must never forget.

Appendix

Statements of Leaders of The Church of Jesus Christ of Latter-day Saints

In this appendix, I have included a selection of statements by leaders of The Church of Jesus Christ of Latter-day Saints (hereafter "Church") on abortion.[129] In the 1970s, around the time the decision of *Roe v. Wade* was announced, the Church often spoke out against unwarranted abortions. However, in recent years, the Church has not continued to speak out about it as much. But the Church's position has not changed. It is helpful to take a moment to review what the Church's position is and to review the statements of some of its leaders during the past fifty years. Here are some of those statements.

In 1973, following the ruling by the Supreme Court in *Roe v. Wade*, the Church issued a statement about abortion in a *Priesthood Bulletin*:

> In view of a recent decision of the United States Supreme Court, we feel it necessary to restate the

---

[129] While this appendix addresses statements by leaders of The Church of Jesus Christ of Latter-day Saints, it is also important for a much broader audience. It is understood that many Christian denominations will have a similar historical background in addressing abortion and fetal rights issues. But there is no need to present a full history of all of them. It is sufficient to merely discuss the background of one—the one with which I am familiar—which can represent a type of religious opposition to and conflict with the *Roe v. Wade* decision.

position of the church on abortion in order that there be no misunderstanding of our attitude.

The church opposes abortion and counsels its members not to submit to or perform an abortion except in the rare cases where, in the opinion of competent medical counsel, the life or good health of the mother is seriously endangered or where the pregnancy was caused by rape and produces serious emotional trauma in the mother. Even then it should be done only after counseling with the local presiding priesthood authority and after receiving divine confirmation through prayer.

I am not aware that the Church ever announced its support of any particular, proposed amendment to the Constitution to protect fetal life. Nevertheless, it is clear from what its various leaders have stated that the Church supports the position that a fetus has a right to live from the moment of conception.

In October 1976, at his opening address at the Church's General Conference, President Spencer W. Kimball characterized abortion as the "destruction of life" and "the taking of life."[130] It would seem to follow that abortion is wrong because it is a species of killing human life.

The Church does not equate abortion with murder, but the First Presidency emphasized that this should not "be construed to minimize the seriousness of this revolting sin."[131] Elder James E. Faust, in a General Conference address, advocated defending and protecting fetal life without any mention as to whether or not the spirit has entered the fetus's body.[132] (As was discussed earlier, the

---

[130] President Spencer W. Kimball, "A Report and a Challenge," *Ensign*, November 1976, pp. 5–6.

[131] *Priesthood Bulletin*, 1973.

[132] *Ensign*, May 1975, p. 29.

quickening distinction is irrelevant to whether the fetal right to life should be recognized.) Elder Faust said:

> Some say, as did the Supreme Court of the United States, that it is only a theory that human life is present from conception. This is contrary to insurmountable medical evidence. Dr. Bernard N. Nathanson recently revealed that he was among those who were militantly outspoken in favor of legalized abortion and joined in using every device available in political action to promote it. He helped set up and became director of the first and largest abortion clinic in the western world. After the center had performed some sixty thousand abortions, Dr. Nathanson resigned as director. He said, "I am deeply troubled by my own increasing certainty that I had in fact presided over 60,000 deaths. There is no longer serious doubt in my mind that human life exists within the womb from the very onset of pregnancy." (*New England Journal of Medicine*, vol. 291, no. 22, p. 1189.)
>
> Way back in the sixteenth century, Arantius showed that maternal and fetal circulations were separate, thus clearly demonstrating that there are two separate lives involved. The unborn babe is certainly alive, because it possesses the token of life which is the ability to reproduce dying cells. (Dr. Eugene F. Diamond, *Illinois Medical Journal*, May 1967).[133]

One of the most evil myths of our day is that a woman who has joined hands with God in creation can destroy that creation because she claims the right

---

[133] In the 1970s, the First Presidency produced a film strip presentation, *Very Much Alive*, which affirmed the existence of life from conception. These two paragraphs from Elder Faust's address are quoted and endorsed in the film strip.

to control her own body. Since the life within her is not her own, how can she justify its termination ...? ... These ... are entitled to a defense in their unborn, natural state of existence.[134]

The Church has never conditioned the sin of abortion on the spirit being in the fetal body. Neither should the secular law make such a distinction.

In recent years, the Church has rarely spoken about the propriety of using contraceptives. However, as late as 1969, the Church discouraged the use of contraceptives except to help the health of the mother. A letter dated April 14, 1969, from the First Presidency to Church leaders included the following statement:

> We seriously regret that there should exist a sentiment or feeling among members of the Church to curtail the birth of their children. We have been commanded to multiply and replenish the earth that we may have joy and rejoicing in our posterity.
>
> Where husband and wife enjoy health and vigor and are free from impurities that would be entailed upon their posterity, it is contrary to the teachings of the Church artificially to curtail or prevent the birth of children. We believe that those who practice birth control will reap disappointment by and by.
>
> However, we feel that men must be considerate of their wives who bear the greater responsibility not only of bearing children, but of caring for them through childhood To this end the mother's health and strength should be conserved and the husband's consideration for his wife is his first duty, and self-control a dominant factor in all their relationships.

---

[134] *Ensign*, May 1976, pp. 28–29.

While the Church condemns most abortions except in certain rare instances to protect the mother or for serious fetal deformities, I am not aware or any Church discipline for the use of contraceptives.

There are several circumstances where it may be difficult to determine whether something is a contraceptive or an abortifacient. Some people may be uncomfortable to even read these next few sentences. According to Obstetrician Paul E. Lewis, the IUD and some birth control pills prevent fertilizations about 90 percent of the time, but in a small percentage of cases, fertilization occurs, after which the IUD or the pill prevent the fertilized egg from implanting in the mother's womb. In those cases, the IUD or pill serve to facilitate the embryo's death, as it cannot survive unless it implants. In such instances, the IUD and the pill do not technically function as contraceptives because they don't prevent conception; both lead to the fertilized egg being discharged from the woman's body. Nevertheless, many if not most people in our society do not usually regard these devises as abortifacients. I am not aware of any statement by the Church with regard to the propriety or not of IUDs and birth control pills.

Whatever the answer is to the above issue, it certainly illustrates the thorny issues that would come to the fore if a constitutional amendment should establish a fetal right to life from the moment of conception.

Some feel that because they are not directly affected by liberalized abortion, it does not matter what the law happens to be. This approach is wrong because these laws do affect us, at least indirectly. And further, we have an obligation to help our brothers and sisters to embrace godly principles and to avoid bad practices.

President Spencer W. Kimball urged members of the Church to "become actively and relentlessly engaged in the fight against this insidious enemy of humanity [pornography] around the world."[135] What President Kimball said regarding opposing pornography also

---

[135] *Ensign*, November 1976, p. 5.

applies to opposing abortion. Members of the Church have taken upon themselves the name of Christ and covenanted to be witnesses for Him at all times, in all places, and in all things. They have a duty to be a light to the world, to be the salt of the earth, and to have a leavening influence on the world. In the Lord's Prayer, Jesus suggested that we pray: "Thy will be done on earth, as it is in heaven" (Matthew 6:10). If we take this suggestion seriously, we will pray and work to bring this condition into existence. It is a virtue to stand up for the right and to exert one's influence to establish principles that will be a great benefit for all.[136] There is something good about this.

One example of this was recounted by Elder Gene R. Cook in his General Conference address in April 1976. Elder Cook explained the blessings and benefits that can come when members speak up for true principles on important issues of our day:

> Many members ask, "Elder Cook, it's easy to say, but how do I do it? What can I specifically do now to fulfill my missionary responsibility to warn my neighbors?" May I provide you with two general suggestions.
>
> First, you can stand up for the truth wherever you are, at all times and in all places. Sometimes our members are fearful to speak up for the truth in clubs, associations, or even, at times, among the members of the Church. As the Lord has said, it should be done with boldness but not overbearance. Speak out for the Lord and for his prophet on the vital issues of the day.
>
> For example, I know of a woman, a good woman, who found herself in a very challenging situation. She was at a luncheon with a number of

---

[136] See, for example, Ezekiel 33:7–9; *Doctrine and Covenants* 24:10; 58:26–29; 82:3; and *Book of Mormon*, Jacob 1:19.

members of the Church; some were active and some inactive; and also a few nonmembers were present. The subject turned to abortion and birth control, and one of the nonmembers voiced for about five minutes some very strong feelings concerning these issues. She indicated, erroneously, that she felt there is nothing wrong with an abortion, and that there should never be any kind of restriction placed on a man or a woman concerning birth control itself. This good sister in the Church was faced with a difficult challenge of whether to talk about the weather or some other noncontroversial subject or whether to really speak out and state the truth. This choice woman chose to do the latter. After explaining what the Lord had said concerning both of those issues, she bore her testimony as to her personal feelings. As you might expect, the luncheon concluded rather abruptly. However, afterwards one of the inactive women came over to this good sister and explained that she had never before understood the Lord's view on those issues and had felt the truth being spoken on that day.

Feel free, when prompted, my brothers and sisters, to bear your testimony of those principles that you know to be true. Sincere feelings conveyed from heart to heart by means of testimony convert people to the truth where weak, wishing-washy argumentative statements will not. (*Ensign*, May 1976, p. 103)

It is both a responsibility and an opportunity to influence others for good. Joseph Smith said: "I feel it to be my right and privilege to obtain what power and influence I can, lawfully, ... for the protection of injured innocence.[137] The very essence of the Gospel teaches that serving others is self-fulfilling and brings the greatest happiness in life. Helping to promote good laws is one example of such service. Members of the Church have a duty to promote righteousness by being influential citizens. Joseph Smith said: "It is our duty to consecrate all our influence to make popular that which is sound and good, and unpopular that which is unsound. It is right, politically, for a man who has influence to use it, as well as for a man who has no influence to use his. From henceforth I will maintain all the influence I can get."[138]

In 1844, Apostle John Taylor said:

> Certainly if any person ought to interfere in political matters it should be those whose minds and judgments are influenced by correct principles— religious as well as political; otherwise those persons professing religion would have to be governed by those who make no professions; be subject to their rule; have the law and word of God trampled under foot, and become as wicked as Sodom and as corrupt as Gomorrah, and be prepared for final destruction.[139]

The Church's 1976–1977 Melchizedek Priesthood manual challenged priesthood bearers to "seek to use [their] influence to promote good government according to [their] own skills, circumstances, and community needs."[140] About this, Joseph Smith made these additional comments:

---

[137] *History of the Church*, 6:210–211.

[138] *History of the Church*, 5:286.

[139] *Times and Seasons*, March 15, 1844.

[140] *My Errand from the Lord*, p. 186.

If I esteem mankind to be in error, shall I bear them down? No. I will lift them up, and in their own way too, if I cannot persuade them my way is better; and I will not seek to compel any man to believe as I do, only by the force of reasoning, for truth will cut its own way.[141]

---

[141] *History of the Church*, 5:499.

Bibliography and Authorities

Bibliography

Basler, ed., *Collected Works of Abraham Lincoln*, vol. 2. (1953).

Benson, Ezra Taft, Conference Address, *Ensign* (Salt Lake City, May and November 1976).

Congressional Quarterly (Aug. 28 and Sept. 18, 1976).

Cook, Gene R., Conference Address, *Ensign*. (May 1976).

Coulter, Ann., *Godless—The Church of Liberalism* (New York: Crown Publishing Group, 2006).

Daily Herald (Provo, UT: Dec. 7, 19, 26, & 31, 1976; and Jan. 13 and Mar. 20, 1977).

Destro, Robert A., "Abortion and the Constitution: The Need for a Life-Protective Amendment," *California L. Rev.* (1975).

de Tocqueville, Alexis, *Democracy in America*, (translated by Henry Reeve), vol. II, book 3 (New York: Schocken Books, 1961).

Doctrine and Covenants (Salt Lake City: The Church of Jesus Christ of Latter-day Saints, 1979).

Ely, "The Wages of Crying Wolf: A Comment on Roe v. Wade," 82 *Yale L. J.* (1973).

Faust, James E., Conference Address, *Ensign* (May, 1976).

Ford, ed., *The Writings of Thomas Jefferson*, vol. VIII (1897).

Gorby, John D., "Introduction to the Translation of the Abortion Decision of the Federal Constitutional Court of the Federal Republic of Germany," *The John Marshall Journal of Practice and Procedure*, vol. 9 (1976).

Greenwood, Ned H., *Human Environment and Natural Systems* (Belmont, California: Wadsworth Publishing Co., 1973).

Gunther, Gerald, "The Supreme Court 1971 Term: A Model for a New Equal Protection," 86 *Harvard L. Rev.* (November 1972). Foote, Levy and Sander, *Cases and Materials on Family Law*, 2nd ed. (Boston: Little, Brown and Company, 1976).

Guttmacher Institute, www.guttmacher.org.

Hopkin, William R., Jr., "Roe v. Wade and the Traditional Legal Standards Concerning Pregnancy," *Temple Law Quarterly*, (1973–74).

Jennings, Scott, "Ralph Northam should be remembered for advocating the slaughtering of deformed babies," *USA Today*, Feb. 5, 2019.

Kelley, Brian H., "On Legislating Morality" (unpublished paper, Oct. 19, 1976).

Kimball, Spencer W., "A Report and a Challenge," *Ensign*, Nov., 1976.

Lewis, Paul E., M.D., interview on May 9, 2020.

National Right to Life Center, nrlc.org.

Padover, Saul K., *The Living U. S. Constitution* (New York: Mentor Books, 1963).

Planned Parenthood, "Margaret Sanger—Our Founder," accessed May 9, 2020 at https://www.plannedparenthood.org/files/9214/7612/8734/Sanger_Fact_Sheet_Oct_2016.pdf .

Prosser, W., *Handbook of the Law of Torts* (4th ed. 1971).

Richardson, ed., *Messages and Papers of the Presidents*, vol. II (1896).

Senate Subcommittee on Health, Committee on Labor and Public Welfare, U. S. Senate 93rd Congress, *Fetal Research* (July 19, 1974).

Silverstein, Elliott, "From Comstockery through Population Control: The Inevitability of Balancing," *N. C. Central L. J.* (Fall 1974).

Smith, Harmon L., *Ethics and New Medicine* (Nashville: Abingdon Press, 1970).

Tanner, N. Eldon, *Conference Report* (Salt Lake City: October, 1965).

Taylor, John, *Times and Seasons* (March 15, 1844).

The Church of Jesus Christ of Latter-day Saints, *Priesthood Bulletin*, 1973.

_____ *History of the Church* (1949).

_____ *My Errand from the Lord* (Melchizedek Priesthood Manual, 1976–1977).

_____ *The Book of Mormon* (Salt Lake City, Utah: 1981).

_____ *The Doctrine and Covenants* (Salt Lake City: 1981).

_____ *Times and Seasons* (Nauvoo, IL: 1844).

_____ *Very Much Alive* [film strip] (1970s).

The First Presidency, letter of April 14, 1969.

The Holy Bible (King James Version).

The Washington Times (February 25, 2004).

United States Commission on Civil Rights, "Constitutional Aspects of the Right to Limit Childbearing" (Washington, DC, 1975).

United States Constitution.

Webster's New World Dictionary of the American Language, Second College Ed. (William Collins + World Publishing Co., Inc., 1978).

Wilke, Dr. and Mrs. J. C., Handbook on Abortion (Cincinnati: Hayes Pub. Co., 1975).

Williams, Armstrong, "Marriage Rites and Civil Rights," *The Washington Times* (February, 2004).

Wilson, John P., "A Report on Legal Issues Involved in Research on the Fetus," *Appendix—Research on the Fetus*, The National Commission for the Protection of Human Subjects of Biomedical and Behavioral Research (HEW) (1976).

Supreme Court Cases

Gonzalez v. Carhart, 550 U.S. 124 (2007): 80

Gregg v. Georgia, 428 U.S. 153 (1976): 10

Griswold v. Connecticut, 381 U.S. 479 (1965): 9, 10, 15, 17, 78, 88

Hollingsworth v. Perry, 570 U.S. 693 (2013): 86

Jacobson v. Massachusetts, 197 U.S. 11 (1905): 51, 64

Lawrence v. Texas, 539 U.S. 558 (2003): 40, 82, 85

Liverpool, New York and Philadelphia Steamship Co. v. Commissioners of
    Emigration, 113 U.S. 33 (1885): 8

Lochner v. New York, 198 U.S. 45 (1905): 38, 87

Maher v. Roe, 432 U.S. 464 (1977): 70

McDonald v. Chicago, 561 U.S. 742 (2010): 40

Obergefell v. Hodges, 576 U.S. ___ (2015): 40, 82, 87

Paris Adult Theatre I v. Slaton, 413 U.S. 49 (1973): 69

Planned Parenthood v. Casey, 505 U.S. 833 (1992): 73, 77

Planned Parenthood of Central Missouri v. Danforth, 428 U.S. 52 (1976):
    34, 60, 71, 72, 73, 76

Reynolds v. United States, 98 U.S. 145 (1878): 51

Roe v. Wade, 410 U.S. 113 (1973): throughout

Roth v. United States, 354 U.S. 476 (1957): 34, 68

Santa Clara County v. Southern Pacific R. R., 118 U.S. 394 (1886): 12

United States v. O'Brien, 391 U.S. 367 (1968): 85

United States v. Windsor, 570 U.S. 744 (2013): 40, 83-87

Webster v. Reproductive Health Services, 492 U.S. 490 (1989): 1, 34, 76-79,
    94, 109

Federal Statutes

18 U.S.C. § 1531   Partial-Birth Abortion Ban Act: 73, 80, 136

Federal Court Cases

Bonbrest v. Kotz, 65 F. Supp. 183 (D.D.C. 1946): 21

Doe v. Commonwealth's Attorney, 403 F. Supp. 1199 (E. D. Va. 1975): 82

Friendship Medical Center, Ltd. v. Chicago Board of Health, 505 F.2d 1141 (7th Cir. 1974): 73

Wagner v. Gardner, 413 F.2d 267 (1969): 20

State Court Cases

Allaire v. St. Luke's Hospital, 184 Ill. 359, 56 N.E. 638 (1900): 20

Davis v. Davis, 842 S.W.2d 588 (Tenn. Sup. Ct., 1992): 90-94

Dietrich v. Inhabitants of Northampton, 138 Mass. 14 (1884): 20, 28, 99

Endresz v. Friedberg, 24 N.Y.S.2d 478, 248 N.E.2d 901 (1969): 99, 104

Howard v. Lecher, 386 N.Y.S.2d 460 (1976): 99-102

Kelley v. Gregory, 282 App. Div. 542, 125 N.Y.S.2d 696 (1953): 56, 98

Keyes v. Construction Serv., 340 Mass. 633, 165 N.E.2d 912: 104

Memorial Hospital v. Anderson, 42 N.J. 421, cert. denied 377 U.S. 958 (1964): 51

Park v. Chessin, 60 A.D.2d 80 (1977): 97

Park v. Chessin, 387 N.Y.S.2d 204 (1976): 96-106

Piper v. Hoard, 107 N.Y. 73, 13 N.E. 626 (1887): 99

Raleigh Fitkin-Paul Morgan Memorial Hospital v. Anderson, 42 N.J. 421, 201 A.2d 537, cert. denied 377 U.S. 985 (1964): 20

Stallman v. Youngquist, 125 Ill.2d 267, 278, 531 N.E.2d 355 (1988): 75

Stewart v. Long Is. Coll. Hosp., 35 A.D.2d 531, aff'd 30 N.Y.2d 695, 332 N.Y.S.2d 640, 283 N.E.2d 616 (1970): 99-102

Swain v. Bowers, 91 Ind. 307, 158 N.E. 598 (1927): 20

Zepeda v. Zepeda, 41 Ill.App.2d 240, 190 N.E.2d 849 (1963): 98

England Court Cases

Doe v. Clarke, 2H. BI. 399, 126 Eng. Rep. 617: 20

Thelluson v. Woodford, 4 Ves. 277, 31 Eng. Rep. 117: 20

Index

F

fallopian tubes 90
family life 68, 82
family planning 59, 66, 108
Faust, James E. 122, 131
federal funds 109
federalism viii
Federal Marriage Amendment 83, 88
fertilization 26, 27, 28, 90, 125
fetal life 1, 2, 5, 18, 27, 30, 31, 32, 34,
　　35, 36, 38, 41, 43, 55, 64, 72, 74,
　　76, 77, 78, 94, 100, 114, 122
fetal research 29, 133
fetal rights vii, viii, ix, x, xi, 2, 3, 4,
　　5, 6, 7, 10, 11, 12, 13, 15, 16, 17,
　　18, 19, 20, 21, 22, 23, 24, 27, 29,
　　30, 32, 34, 36, 38, 39, 40, 42, 43,
　　50, 52, 53, 54, 55, 56, 58, 59, 61,
　　63, 64, 66, 68, 71, 75, 76, 78, 79,
　　90, 97, 98, 101, 104, 106, 107,
　　112, 113, 114, 115, 118, 119, 121,
　　123, 125
fetal right to life vii, viii, ix, x, xi, 2,
　　3, 4, 5, 6, 7, 10, 11, 12, 13, 16, 17,
　　18, 19, 20, 22, 23, 24, 30, 32, 39,
　　40, 42, 43, 50, 52, 53, 54, 55, 56,
　　58, 59, 61, 63, 64, 68, 71, 75, 76,
　　79, 98, 106, 112, 113, 114, 115,
　　119, 123, 125
Fetal Right-to-Life Amendment 64,
　　107, 112, 118, 119
fetology 25
fetus xi, 2, 3, 7, 11, 12, 14, 16, 17, 19,
　　20, 21, 22, 23, 25, 27, 28, 29, 30,
　　31, 32, 34, 35, 36, 37, 42, 43, 52,
　　56, 58, 60, 61, 63, 72, 73, 75, 76,
　　77, 80, 93, 98, 100, 103, 104, 105,
　　106, 109, 113, 114, 119, 122, 134
Fifth Amendment 85
First Amendment 51, 52, 53, 62, 68

First Presidency 122, 123, 124, 133
Florida 19, 74, 75
fornication 56, 83
Fourteenth Amendment 2, 3, 4, 6, 7,
　　11, 12, 14, 15, 17, 38, 39, 40, 42,
　　55, 56, 62, 63, 73, 82, 103, 119
Fourth Amendment 15, 39
France 5, 26, 91
Frederickson, Dr. Donald 105
free agency 118
freedom of choice 108
freedom of conscience 52
freedom of religion 52
freedom of speech 62
free exercise of religion 52
frozen embryo custody case 90, 94
fruitful and multiply 65
full faith and credit clause 83, 86
fundamental rights 1, 2, 16, 17, 58

G

Gallup Poll 109
gay rights 40, 81, 85
genetic disorder 100
Georgia 1, 10, 16, 19, 105, 134, 135
Germany 5, 132
Ginsburg, Justice Ruth Bader 79
Goldberg, Justice 17
Gomorrah 128
Gorby, John D. 5, 132
Greenwood, Ned 132
Gunther, Gerald 11, 132
Guttmacher Institute x, 119, 132
gynecologist 26, 100

H

Hamilton, Alexander 15
handicapped 13
Harlan, Justice 34, 68
Harvard 4, 11, 66, 132

hatred toward gays 85
health of the mother 8, 122, 124
health requirements 73
Holmes, Oliver Wendell 20
Holocaust x
homosexual conduct vii
Hopkin, William R., Jr. 132
human life x, xi, 1, 2, 7, 23, 25, 26, 28, 32, 40, 42, 55, 63, 64, 68, 76, 77, 93, 99, 108, 114, 115, 119, 120, 122, 123

I

Illinois 19, 32, 75, 98, 110, 123
inalienable rights vii, 15
incest 57, 58, 70, 107, 112, 114
Indiana 19
inheritance 20, 98, 99
in vitro fertilization 90
Iowa 19
irreconcilable differences 91
IRS 84
Italy 5
IUD 125
IVF 90, 91, 93, 94. *See* in vitro fertilization

J

Jackson, Andrew 41, 42
Jefferson, Thomas 41, 42, 132
Jews x
judicial activism 83
judicial branch 8, 41
judicial legislation viii, 7, 8
judicial power viii, 33
judicial restraint viii, 7, 77, 86, 87

K

kangaroos 29

Kansas 19
Kelley, Brian H. 117, 132
Kennedy, Edward 29
Kennedy, Justice Anthony 79, 83
Kentucky 19
Kimball, Spencer W. 122, 125, 132
King, Dr. I. Ray 91
Kissinger, Henry 66
Korea 69

L

lack of judicial restraint viii, 7
legislating morality 116, 117, 132
legislative branch 10, 41
Lewis, Paul E., MD 69, 125
"liberty" under Fifth Amendment 85
Life magazine 62
Lincoln, Abraham 41, 42, 131
"living Constitution" 39
Los Angeles Times 109
Louisiana 19, 24
Louisiana State Med. Society 24

M

male chauvinism 14
malice toward gays 85
marital deduction 84
marriage viii, 13, 16, 30, 40, 57, 67, 81, 82, 83, 84, 86, 87, 88, 89, 134
Marshall, Justice John 5, 39, 132
Marshall, Justice Thurgood 79
marsupials 28, 29
Maryland 19
Massachusetts 19, 51, 64, 135
McCain, John 110
meaningful life 36, 61
mechanical womb 94
mental distress 100, 101
mercy killing 60
Michigan 19, 108

Q

quality of life 75, 98, 105
quick or quickening 54, 123

R

rape 57, 58, 59, 70, 107, 111, 112,
    114, 122
Reagan, Ronald 107, 109, 112
referendum 86
refund 84
Rehnquist, Justice William 116
religious beliefs 2, 53
reproductive freedom 108
reproductive health 1, 76, 94, 108, 109,
    134, 135
reproductive rights 62
Revelle, Roger 66
reverse *Roe* 76
right not to be conceived 96, 97,
    101, 102
right not to be pregnant 56, 57, 58
right to bear arms 40
right to life vii, viii, ix, x, xi, 2, 3, 4, 5,
    6, 7, 10, 11, 12, 13, 15, 16, 17, 18,
    19, 20, 22, 23, 24, 26, 27, 28, 30,
    32, 36, 37, 39, 40, 42, 43, 50, 52,
    53, 54, 55, 56, 58, 59, 60, 61, 63,
    64, 68, 69, 71, 72, 75, 76, 79, 93,
    97, 98, 103, 105, 106, 110, 112,
    113, 114, 115, 119, 123, 125, 132
right to limit childbearing 41, 50, 63,
    64, 109, 133
right to privacy vii, x, 1, 2, 6, 11, 12,
    15, 16, 38, 39, 54, 75, 82, 113, 119
right to Social Security benefits 20
right to unlimited childbearing 63, 65
Roberts, Justice John 87
Robertson, Dr. John 92
Rockefeller, Gov. Nelson 1

Roe, Jane 8
Roe v. Wade vii, viii, ix, x, xi, 1, 2, 5, 6,
    7, 8, 18, 19, 21, 24, 28, 29, 31, 32,
    33, 39, 63, 70, 71, 72, 74, 75, 76,
    77, 78, 79, 80, 83, 89, 92, 93, 97,
    103, 107, 108, 110, 111, 112, 113,
    114, 119, 121, 131, 132, 135
Romney, Mitt 111
Roosevelt, Franklin D. 41

S

saline amniocentesis 72
same-sex marriage viii, 40, 81, 82, 83,
    86, 87, 88, 89
Sanger, Margaret 62, 132
Scalia, Justice Antonin 74, 76, 78, 84,
    85, 86
Second Amendment 40
selective incorporation 40
selfishness 68
separation of church and state 51, 52
sexual intercourse 13, 57, 58, 60
sexual relations viii, 57, 81, 82
Smith, Harmon L. 27, 133
Smith, Joseph 127, 128
social effects of abortion 67
social security 16, 20
Sodom 128
sodomy 81–83
Souter, Justice 74
South Carolina 19
spiritual life 26, 52, 56
spousal consent 71
standing 83, 84, 86, 103, 104
Stevens, Justice 78
Stewart, Justice 3, 116
stillborn child 22
substantive due process 38, 87
suction abortion 26

About the Author

C. Paul Smith has had a general law practice in Maryland for over 40 years. He has also been an elected official in Frederick County, Maryland. He is also the author of *The State of the Constitution – 2017*; *The Capitalism Argument* (2019); *I Will Send My Messenger* (1988, 2019), and *The Prophet Joseph Smith – Restoration Issues* (2019). See his website: www.cpaulsmith.com.

Lightning Source UK Ltd.
Milton Keynes UK
UKHW041053231120
373920UK00001B/44